A COMMON CURRICULUM:
the case of Northern Ireland.

Edited by Leslie Caul

First published in 1993

Published by
LRU Stranmillis College
Belfast
BT9 5DY.

British Library Cataloguing in Publication Data
A COMMON CURRICULUM.
1. Northern Ireland. Curriculum
1. Caul Leslie

Contents

LIST OF CONTRIBUTORS

Alan Robinson is a lecturer at the University of Ulster

Alexander McEwen is a senior lecturer at the School of Education, Queen's University, Belfast

Samuel McGuffin is a senior tutor at Stranmillis College, Belfast.

John Gardiner is a reader at the School of Education, Queen's University, Belfast

Pat McNally is a teacher in Belfast

Clifford Boyd is a senior lecturer at Stranmillis College, Belfast

Martin Fitzpatrick is a senior lecturer at Stranmillis College, Belfast

Barbara Erwin is a senior tutor at Stranmillis College, Belfast

Gertrude Patterson is a principal lecturer at Stranmillis College, Belfast

Leslie Caul is a principal lecturer at Stranmillis College, Belfast

List of Abbreviations

APU	Assessment of Performance Unit
ASE	Association for Science Education
DENI	Department of Education for Northern Ireland
DES	Department of Education and Science
EC	European Communities
EcATT	Economic Awareness Teacher Training Programme
EHSSB	Eastern Health and Social Services Board
ELB	Education and Library Board
EMU	Education for Mutual Understanding
HEC	Health Education Council
NCC	National Curriculum Council
NICED	Northern Ireland Council for Educational Development
NICSE	Northern Ireland Certificate of Secondary Education
NISCC	Northern Ireland Schools Curriculum Committee
OPCS	Office of Population Censuses and Surveys
PSE	Personal and social education
SACHR	Standing Advisory Council on Human Rights
SC/HEC	Schools Council/Health Education Council
SCHEP	Schools Council Health Education Projects
SHEG	Scottish Health Education Group
SSCR	Secondary Science Curriculum Review
TACADE	Teacher's Council on Alcohol and Drug Education
WHO	World Health Organisation

EDUCATION IN NORTHERN IRELAND: the case for curriculum

Leslie Caul

Education in Northern Ireland is, in its classroom practices, both similar to and different from that in the rest of the United Kingdom. While classrooms may be relatively similar within the British Isles and, indeed throughout most of the developed world, individual differences in organisation and in the delivery of the curriculum can create subtle variations in the pattern of experiences children have throughout their school careers. If not actually trapped by their histories, schools have become heavily influenced by the established pattern of educational experiences provided to earlier generations. As in all other aspects of life, history has been remarkably influential in shaping people's lives in this province where most social experience has been constructed in a divided state struggling for an identity among its cultural legacies. In Northern Ireland while one cultural group denies its local history and looks to Britain for a common identity, the other celebrates its Irishness as a mark of separation and distinctiveness. In education this has led inevitably to a dual system of schools that acclaims differing identities and does as more to separate the two cultural identities than to unite them.

It is not only the pattern of control and affiliation but the organisation of the school system that differentiates schooling in Northern Ireland. At first glance the contemporary basis of schooling followed the British model from 1947 when schools were distinguished by attainment and potential academic achievement creating a system built on differentiation by ability. The British reforms of the 1960s however failed to penetrate the bastions of established privilege in Northern Ireland as religious and cultural differences were subsumed to build a 'fortified castle' of selective schools in deference to more liberal educational thought that identified under-achievement as a major problem especially among those children not selected by the 11+ tests. British welfarism floundered in the wake of a privileged minority on both sides of the cultural divide that served to cement the continuation of selective secondary schooling. Education became a means of maintaining two cultures that were adept at the celebration of identities that upheld deep schisms across the province and trapped children into sets of social meanings that were either Irish or British but not both.

From the 1930s education in Northern Ireland has ensured the relative isolation of both cultural groups by maintaining two separate systems of schools. The failure of early Unionist administrations to integrate schools, while not surprising, ensured a Protestant identity to state schools and led to the creation of a separate Catholic system of school administration.

The early 1950s saw the emergence of social class as a potent variable as the selective system provided an ideological link that united the privilege of the selected few in both systems at the expense of the majority. Selection at 11+ created separate designated superior groups of Catholic and Protestant children who were not only divided from the other cultural setting but also from fellow co-religionists who attended a different level of secondary schooling. Both groups on either side of the religious and education divide had available to them a cross-religious link that could not be developed as the two separate but closely parallel school systems continued to develop apart.

The possibility of reorganisation of secondary education was rejected in Northern Ireland as were other innovations by a conservatism articulated by well organised groups representing grammar schools. These groups played on the fears of a population fearful of a loss of privilege in a marginal region with high structural unemployment and slow industrial growth. Schooling therefore remained a source of in-built inequality for many but especially so for girls who, while obtaining higher grades than boys, were discriminated against in the selection tests to ensure equity between the sexes enrolled in grammar schools.

The dual system of schools reflected the bitter ironies of an education service that strove to prepare its charges with the means of combating the rigours of life at the margins of the British economy while maintaining an archaic view of cultural identity. This history of separation served to divide the society while the processes of enough difficulties with the clauses in the structures i so and i have reasons to planning for assessment

education germinated a service that had the appearance of a modern system if the roots of old practice. Nevertheless there are those who would suggest that Britain through the introduction of educational reform and especially the National Curriculum is now recognising its own educational short-comings and returning to the 'golden standards' which have been at the heart of education and its curriculum in this province for the last 50 years.

The management of the curriculum in Northern Ireland has remained an issue for the Department of Education following a tradition of centralised and bureaucratic control. The province did not have a Schools Council but a Curriculum Committee that managed change but increasingly became, because of its location in the Ministry, locked into maintaining a particular system of schools and reinforcing the existing educational structure. This government appointed and managed body retained control and effectively prevented teachers from shaping or experimenting with curriculum change. However a few curriculum initiatives did flourish following the lead of the School's Council but these were mainly in secondary intermediate schools. Grammar school education and the structure that maintained it remained untouched for much of the 1960s-1980s.

Curriculum innovation in the 1980s took its lead from the Northern Ireland Council for Educational Development (NICED). A centrally designed and managed council proposed two main initiatives in this period. Firstly NICED produced a series of primary school curriculum guidelines based on subjects in the primary school curriculum. Secondly the council piloted a programme of secondary school based curriculum review on a whole school review model. This scheme became the 11-16 Programme. TRAWL and LAMP followed existing English models as subordinates to the main initiatives. A Centre for Educational Management provided a programme for training school principals in the running of their schools again following the lead given by the Department. Through a period of innovation and expansion in the schools the universities were notable by their absence except when firstly contributions from Professor Skilbeck at the University of Ulster and Professor Rex Cathcart at Further Professional Studies at Queen's became influential in the debate about educational change. Cultural reconstruction became an intellectual theme for expansion in the universities' Schools of Education in the 1970s only to be met with a defiant stance from Education and Library Boards, the only form of local authority left after local government reform in the 1970s. Thus the paramount selective educational structures remained impervious to change throughout the 1980's.

There are important ideological differences between education in Northern Ireland and that in Great Britain. The retention of selection and the continual dominance of the grammar school have created a system of schools that have an in-built model of excellence that perpetuates and permeates a society that depends a great deal upon its schools for a level of stability. It is the subtle catigorisation of pupils that provides those reference points that inform citizens of their identity. In the province identity takes only one form, 'Catholic' or 'Protestant' not both. Cultural identity is reinforced through the outcomes of education that because of the deeply divided nature of the society requires a sharp and decisive definition of social identity. Having school types sharply marked by ability allowed deep schisms to open across a society closely referenced to what school an individual attended through a school career. It was in outcomes that Northern Ireland differed sharply from the rest of in the United Kingdom. The existence of grammar schools allows the province to rely on these schools for its academic reputation. The performance of other types of schools rarely enter the debate about educational standards.

Educational performance in Northern Ireland is regarded as good at the age of 11 in the areas of mathematics and language. It was less reassuring at age 15 and least reassuring in science, for which provision in schools was found to be inadequate at all age levels and in which performance was seen to fall off with age. While the unevenness of provision in schools was found unacceptable it lent support for a notion that APU evidence was incomplete in two respects. The APU national and regional comparisons are presented in terms of average performance with less attention to the range of achievement. As a consequence there has been little attempt to locate the problem of under-achievement in the Northern Ireland school system beyond what can be inferred by association.

The School Leavers data are more revealing with regard to academic outcomes. This data has made it clear that not only is Northern Ireland unusual in its profile of performance but also that profile is a direct reflection of its system of secondary schools. There is a greater than usual proportion of school leavers with good 'A' level results in the grammar school system and a disproportionate number of leavers with no qualifications coming from the secondary intermediate sector. In particular SACHR has drawn attention to the *School Leavers Survey* (1989) where it was reported that in 1989 12.7% of those leaving school had no qualifications. This compares with an overall proportion of 7.9% in England and Wales. The *SACHR Report* (1989-1992) quoted its consultants in showing that the most significant factor as the proportion of unqualified males leaving maintained secondary modern schools: *the significant minority of maintained (ie Catholic) schools where a very high proportion on male leavers are unqualified* (para 12). This disproportionate representation from maintained schools remains a significant and important factor in identifying under-achievement in Northern Ireland.

In Northern Ireland the selective grammar school is expected to achieve academic results. Since it is less clear what the secondary school is expected to achieve it may be concluded that such schools have developed by default using the widely accepted model of so called academic excellence. It is only fair to ask what role the secondary school is to play in the 1990's? And especially so when it will be expected to present all its 14 and 16 year olds for assessment in the subjects of the common curriculum.

The inability of the Northern Ireland school system to facilitate or accept change led inevitably to reform in the late 1980s. Political reluctance to change from within the system itself led to the imposition of a form of British conservatism. The argument for the retention of the existing structures of the school system was based on the achievement rates of abler pupils as indices of success. However the reluctance of the education service to accept a need for reform led directly to one being imposed from Westminster.

This reform was based on the British model but it reflected those particular aspects of education that are characterised as Northern Irish. Strong arguments were proposed to suggest that education in Northern Ireland was in need of fine tuning and not such radical reform. Nevertheless the curriculum was restructured to include those elements seen as important in England and Wales save in some respect where an attempt was made to broaden the primary school curriculum by the compulsory addition of science, history, geography and asthetic subjects including art and physical education. However the Northern Irish dimension was added to the curriculum by including Cultural Heritage and EMU (Education For Mutual Understanding) as cross-curricular themes. In this way a distinct curriculum emerged that proposed to address the cultural divide through the compulsory imposition of school exchange visits and common programmes of study among differing religious groups. Other cross-curricular themes address issues that are important to the economic well-being of the province and include IT, health education and economic awareness.

This book explores the Northern Ireland curriculum posing the question, what is essentially different about the delivery of knowledge in the curriculum in Northern Ireland? What makes the curriculum Northern Irish? Two lines of exploration follow: one looks at the cross curricular themes analysing their content and delivery; a second theme explores the core of the curriculum and provides an analysis of English, mathematics and science.

EDUCATION FOR MUTUAL UNDERSTANDING (EMU)

Alan Robinson

INTRODUCTION

As the Common Curriculum begins to be implemented in Northern Ireland in 1990/91 there are few teachers who have not met 'EMU' in one form or other. Responses to what one teacher has called 'a policy of EMU-isation' naturally vary from expressions of missionary zeal to total rejection, but the bulk of teachers appear to accept it. In the Western Education and Library Board area, Bullick (1990) found that 68% of principal teachers/schools were *convinced of the value of EMU* and that as few as 13% of principal teachers/schools *remain to be convinced of its value*. Of the 22 respondents to the Department of Education's consultative report on EMU, only one was 'totally opposed' to it (Northern Ireland Curriculum Council; 1989, 5).

Before teachers begin to reflect upon - and possibly, defend - the EMU experiences and activities they must generate in the 1990s, it is prudent (a) to examine what EMU is (the concept), (b) to know how EMU might be done (its pedagogy) and (c) to realise that if EMU is to remain a part of the common curriculum at the end of the century, evidence will have to be collected on the progress of teachers and pupils in schools (assessment and evaluation). As it is premature to address the last fully, the purpose of this chapter is to further an awareness of EMU and to promote improved EMU practice among teachers.

EDUCATION FOR MUTUAL UNDERSTANDING AS A CONCEPT

The Northern Ireland Curriculum Council (NICC) has adopted a definition of EMU set out by the Working Group to the Northern Ireland Department of Education (1989,5):

EMU is about self-respect, and respect for others, and the improvement of relationships between people of differing cultural traditions.

This definition is based upon several assumptions that were addressed by teachers involved in earlier curriculum research and development; the most fundamental of these is the view that teachers, most of whom work in schools that are overwhelmingly segregated by cultural tradition and expressed variously as Catholic /Nationalist/ Republican on the one hand and Protestant/Unionist/ Loyalist on the other, can develop an overt ameliorating curriculum for a divided society in conflict. Drawing upon that experience the members of the Department of Education's Working Group noted the danger that too much may be expected of schools but they were unanimous in the conviction that EMU is *essential and deserving of massive public support* (letter to the government minister with responsibility for education from the chairman of the Working Group; 24/4/89).

The definition of EMU features the concepts of 'respect' and 'relationships' and it follows that the lack of respect (normally thought to arise from low self-esteem and poor relationships would account for the existing level of mutual misunderstanding among the population. The perception of oneself and of others is an important consideration (see, for example, O'Donnell 1977).

The key concept, however, of all planned programmes of EMU within schools and between schools has to be 'mutuality'. It is suggested that mutuality is a way individuals and groups relate together respectfully as equals to undertake common educational tasks. The process involves the dismantling of overlapping barriers that get in the way of better relationships and improved understanding and the challenge to teachers (and others) is formidable. These barriers may be manifest by various expressions of prejudice and common sectarianism but they comprised (a) the so-called baggage of hurtful personal experience and early biography - in and out of school (b) the repeated reception of ignorant or dogmatic expression concerning local and wider social, economic and political issues and structures and (c) feelings of superiority arising from ethnocentricity, false pride and unreal external threat. Mutuality begins with an awareness that the images held of others might have been imposed by family, peers, church and elected leaders, the media, teachers and others; they have not normally been arrived at by the young in an unbiased setting. Education cannot be value free but it could provide the most favourable setting for the barriers in the way of mutual understanding to be removed.

It would be a mistake to consider these barriers as being external to schooling and curriculum. If schools are now deemed by government to be part of a wider solution to existing misunderstandings then teachers have to recognise that they might have been - and could remain - part of the problem. EMU causes all teachers to review their relationships with their pupils, to press for appropriate policy in their schools and to monitor their practice. *EMU*, said one at the end of an In-Service course, *is like infilling the Grand Canyon with a spoon; but we shall never treat children the same again.* Mutuality can grow if teachers (and others) can create opportunities for pupils to learn more about themselves, to study and talk about issues of concern to them and to the community, to learn more about others who may be as similar as they are different, and, above all, to achieve together.

The Circular 21 issued by the Department of Education in 1982 was the first public recognition that this kind of liberation could, and should, be facilitated by teachers within the formal education system;

every teacher, every school manager, Board member and trustee, and every educational administrator within the system has a responsibility for helping children to learn to understand and respect each other, and their differing customs and traditions, and of preparing them to live together in harmony in adult life,

Before the evolution of EMU within the teaching profession over a twenty year period is traced, there is some wisdom in stating what EMU is not. The EMU Guide prepared by the former Northern Ireland Council for Educational Development (1988,10) touches on this: for instance it is not a threat to particular traditions and cultures; it is not an attack on segregated education; it is not a form of propaganda exercise by which children are trained in what to believe; and it is not a cosmetic activity on the injustices of society. The authors of the Guide state rather that EMU is designed to encourage, respect and esteem for all, that EMU works within the existing structures, that EMU is about the opening of minds to the importance of diversity and pluralism and that EMU should begin a process that might start to address the wider problems connected with political and economic discrimination that has in turn created a society of dominant and subordinate groups (see Northern Ireland Curriculum Council 1989,4). In a successful democratic society all good education would be directed towards such ends.

An analysis of the origin and evolution of EMU provides a further insight into this cross-curricular theme. Three phases may be identified; these are (a) the research and development phase largely of the 1970s, (b) the policy and support phase of the 1980s and (c) the unfolding current government reform phase.

The research and development phase (1970-81) highlights the initiative from within the professional ranks that followed the onset of the violence and civil unrest in 1968/9. Three educationists - namely John Malone, Malcolm Skilbeck and Tony Spencer - made different analyses of schooling and society and pressed for different educational responses none of which have been successfully achieved, but in so doing, each has made a contribution to EMU being a statutory requirement of the Common Curriculum.

The late John Malone was seconded from Orangefield Boys School in 1970 to investigate what schools could do about community relations in Northern Ireland. In his report Schools Project in Community Relations (1972) he rejected the structural integration of schools in effect as being of less importance that the comprehensivisation of post-primary schools, but he accepted the need for a moral education that would enable pupils to become more considerate towards, and tolerant of, each other and for a cultural education that would enable them to learn more about the history, customs, traditions and common values of Northern Ireland associated with the writings of Estyn Evans (1970) and the work and spirit of Terence O'Neill represented by the then recently opened Ulster Folk Museum at Cultra. He argued that schools themselves must radically change their whole approach to learning if they were to make a lasting contribution to a more humane society. His

Schools Curriculum Project (1973-78) involved many teachers in curriculum developments in a number of areas and the Schools Support Service (1978-82) attempted to assist whole schools to change. After John Malone's untimely death, whole school curriculum review was to provide a neglected or under-used context for the promotion of EMU within Northern Ireland post-primary schools.

The second contribution was that of Malcolm Skilbeck who was head of the Education Centre at the former New University of Ulster. His reconstructionist view of education provided a stimulating philosophy that threw teachers into the front line as cultural change agents. He initiated the Schools Cultural Studies Project (1974-80) to increase levels of tolerance and greater degrees of mutual understanding among young people in Northern Ireland and inspired two projects on the teaching of religion (Greer and McElhinney 1984). Like Malone, Skilbeck worked within the segregated system and the Schools Cultural Studies Project featured materials on Northern Ireland, but the Project did not avoid controversial issues and it piloted cross-community contact between pupils on joint-work drawn from maintained and controlled primary and post-primary schools (Robinson 1980).

The third contribution was made by Queen's University, Belfast, sociologist Tony Spencer who along with others founded the 'All Children Together' movement and pressed government for the rights of parents to choose integrated education if they so wished. Spencer claimed that segregated schooling directly reinforced cultural misunderstanding, stereotyping and prejudice and that it perpetuated segregation in marriage, in work, in housing, in politics, recreation and the mass-media. As it obstructs the emergence of a shared identity or cause, he argued that segregated education undermines the social foundations of potential conflict resolution systems (Spencer 1987). It was not the movement's original intention to establish new schools, but difficulties in converting existing schools led it to found its own school (Lagan College) in 1981 (Wilson and Dunn 1989). More recently, integrated schools have stressed that if children are to be prepared for a plural society teachers must create a curriculum that develops a good positive self-image and, like the Schools Cultural Studies Project, a curriculum that includes cross-cultural studies.

The policy and support phase (1982-88) emphasised the role of the formal structures in furthering EMU in the curriculum. The contributions made were associated more with organisations than with individuals - these included the Department of Education, the Northern Ireland Council for Educational Development and the Education and Library Boards.

The phase began with the publication of Circular 21 by the Department of Education; The Contribution of Schools to Community Relations'. This legitimised the pioneering and controversial work arising out of curriculum development projects being undertaken by teachers in formal and non-formal settings. The Circular urged everyone in the education system to further effort *to ensure that children do not grow up in ignorance, fear or even hatred of those from whom they are educationally segregated.* Official responses to this Circular from within the statutory education sector and the voluntary sector led eventually to the more tangible financial support outlined in Circular 1987/47, 'A Cross-Community Contact Scheme' (and the associated Circular 1988/2 that provided the necessary substitute teacher cover for planned EMU activities between schools). The demands made by teachers and youth leaders on this scheme from 1987/8 was helped by a small number of inspectors whose brief was extended to include EMU and it resulted in additional amounts of finance being made available to applicants.

The Northern Ireland Council for Educational Development established an EMU Steering Group in 1983/4. Its membership, broadly representative of the education interests in the province, drafted a policy statement on EMU that the parent Council approved and distributed to every school. By 1988, it had followed this up with a 50 page teachers' guide and accompanying leaflets to assist staff development meetings and schools to inform parents about EMU in a manner that each felt was appropriate.

The Education and Library Boards supported EMU activity in various ways and varying degrees. Some Boards provided covert rather than overt support: after the publication of Circular 21 in 1982, the latter responded by producing their policy statements but the resourcing of any EMU programme arising from them was not consistent. Only one Board seconded a teacher to disseminate its own EMU policy and to work with teachers on specific EMU programmes. The more cautious Boards were not able to produce policy statements but they did quietly provide financial support to any school within their area with teachers sufficiently motivated to be engaged in cross-community joint-work before the announcement of the Cross-Community Contact Scheme by the Department of Education in 1987.

The University of Ulster offered some in-service education on EMU throughout the phase, and, in association with the Western Education and Library Board, its research Centre for the Study of Conflict began an interventionist phase in its work from 1986 by supporting teachers/schools involved with the Inter-School Links Project.

During this period the number of integrated schools in Northern Ireland increased. The parents responsible for this were supported at the formative stage by the Belfast Trust for Integrated Education that advocated a child-centred approach to education. Once such schools were established the financial security that went along with being recognised by the Department of Education as maintained was achieved more smoothly as the decade progressed. It was clear that government approved of them.

The current phase of government reform clearly promotes integrated schooling and Education for Mutual Understanding. It has introduced Grant Maintained Status to encourage and assist any existing school with a commitment to provide for the co-education of Protestant and Roman Catholic children. So far this has attracted the planned integrated schools; other schools who qualify and would benefit have either met local opposition or have held back in the knowledge of such opposition or held back anticipating such opposition or have rejected it totally.

The Education Order (1989) however legislated that EMU form part of the Common Curriculum. Every school is required to provide for the attainment of the objectives of EMU as recommended by the Northern Ireland Curriculum Council:

(i)   *Interdependence: pupils should develop a knowledge and appreciation of interdependence within the family, within the local community and within the wider world.*

(ii)   *Cultural traditions: pupils should develop a knowledge and understanding of the similarities and differences between cultural traditions that influence people who live in Northern Ireland.*

(iii)   *Understanding conflict: pupils should develop a knowledge and understanding of conflict in a variety of contexts and of constructive and non-violent ways of dealing with it.*
        (NICC 1989 pp.15-16)

Ministerial subject working groups, particularly in English, in history and in geography, have drafted statements of attainment cross-referenced with EMU as a cross-curricular theme, and Education and Library Boards have seconded teachers to advise and support their colleagues to adjust to new demands imposed upon them.

The origin and evolution of EMU in any individual school will be unique to that school. It will have developed according to the values, status and energy of teachers and the degree of support afforded them by the school principal, the local Department of Education inspector, the Education and Library Board advisory service and the higher education institutions and will be related to the wider cultural, historical, political, religious and socio-economic context of the local community.

A PEDAGOGY FOR EDUCATION FOR MUTUAL UNDERSTANDING

Standards in EMU work arise from the motivation of teachers who focus their professional action on children, on their subject and upon the community of Northern Ireland. In the course of twenty years of experience in educating for mutual understanding, many have developed a wide range of imaginative activities that constitutes their creative response to conflict and division.   Three broad approaches or emphases can be identified: these are EMU as personal development, EMU as subject development and EMU as contact.

EMU as personal development: this approach would feature self-respect and esteem. At a whole school level this will normally be found among the stated aims of the school; less commonly it will be the core of a timetabled PSD (Personal and Social Development). Its roots are in progressivist education of the whole child and the key concept is 'identify'. Exemplar materials include titles like 'Who Am I' and strategies include activities that promote affirmation of the individual, co-operation among individuals prejudice reduction and experiential learning that confronts young people with themselves. The Peace Education programmes of the Irish Council of Churches and the Irish Commissioners of Justice and Peace together with the Quaker project based at Magee College led by Jerry Tyrell represent this tradition. Many teachers argue that without a timetabled opportunity to focus directly upon EMU in module form in a PSE programme, any threads of EMU elsewhere cannot be drawn together and consolidated into meaningful and lasting learning.

EMU as subject development: this approach arises out of the contributions that timetabled subjects have increasingly made towards EMU since 1982. Established subjects have accommodated some content and pedagogy of curriculum developments in such areas as Religion in Ireland and Social, Cultural, Community, Political, Local and Environmental Studies. Vivian McIver of the DENI Inspectorate has been one of those associated with the successful application and further development of new approaches piloted in such areas as the subject of history that now bears little resemblance to that challenged by Jack Magee some twenty years ago (Magee, 1970). Materials are more issues based and controversial, but the underlying roots remain academic. The key concept is 'standards'. The social sciences had much to contribute to an understanding of society but in the manner of Peace Education in England, they have been totally rejected as 'wayward' by the current government and educationists have been told that parents do not look for such non-basic learning.

As the common curriculum is subject based this approach must expand further within traditional subjects; the ministerial working group proposals attempt this, but the tensions of accommodating the more controversial practices that can best promote EMU within the compulsory subjects will be formidable and must not be underestimated. For example, central government appears to be bent on rendering history as a less effective force in the promotion of EMU than it might be; a values clarification process that creates the freedom for pupils to choose their opinion and beliefs from the study of alternatives may be obliterated by an imposed process of assessment, and time may not be found for those insightful strategies like role-play and simulation, field work and discussion that form part of the EMU pedagogy.

EMU as contact: this approach stresses the need for improved inter-personal relationships. It has been championed by successive government ministers responsible for education in Northern Ireland since 1982 and it builds upon the joint work generated between pupils attending controlled and maintained schools by the Schools Cultural Studies project and upon the benefits of cross-community residential experiences associated with Corrymeela. Its roots are in reconstructionist education and the key concept is improved 'relationships' (the fourth 'r' in the curriculum). Strategies range from joint sport and carol services and holidays together in neutral places to joint studies of issues facing the community. The widespread use made by the teachers of the DENI Cross-Community Contact Scheme since 1987/8 has demonstrated the commitment of teachers and the need for financial and other support for their work. It has also led to a danger that contact may be contrived by teachers in order to attain goals other than EMU goals.

So prominent has contact become that EMU is mistakenly seen as synonymous with it. EMU is a requirement of the common curriculum; cross-community contact remains an aspiration. NICC has recommended that pupils should have experience of EMU activities with respect to at least one of the following:

(i)   *exploration, within the classroom, of contemporary controversial issues complemented by relevant visitors and visits;*

(ii)   *the exchange of materials especially those reflecting cultural difference, using all forms of communication systems, with the possibility of visits to common ground and to each other's schools;*

(iii)   *joint work extending ultimately to international contact and including the exploration of controversial social and political issues, both local and general.*

In this NICC might appear to be adopting a gradient approach to contact and to an associated controversial content, but face-to-face contact across the divide may be seen as an educational climax of key stage 4 or, strangely, as something to be avoided by teachers and pupils (NICC 1989, 16).

CASE STUDIES OF EDUCATION FOR MUTUAL UNDERSTANDING

Three case studies - one from primary and two from the secondary sector - convey experience and progress; they are reported very much as the teachers involved outlined them. The first and second of these anticipate the current development of EMU as a cross-curricular theme while the third has been selected to represent the reality facing those schools which are required to extend themselves if they are to meet the current objectives of EMU.

1.   Three Small Schools Together

This group of one maintained and two controlled primary schools emerged out of the ELB's local cluster group to formulate school policies based on the Primary Guidelines. It grew to help the schools involved through the quagmire of change and to enable them to exchange resources, references, skills and to formulate policy. Together the staffs saw the common ground of profession, small size and rural location and used it to mutual advantage.

The group soon realised that they had a perfect opportunity to bring together pupils of differing religious and political persuasion. Early pupil contacts were one-off and tentative, such as various sporting fixtures and then outings to the theatre, exhibitions and museums. Any fears at that stage were allayed by the children's responsiveness towards one another; the common ground between them helped to remove any shyness and thoughts of difference between them. Madonna, Bros, Manchester United and Liverpool FC bridged any cultural divide. Conceived through common needs the three small schools found themselves aligned with government policy and in terms of action ahead of any schedule that they might have been able to plan separately.

It was recognised that the teachers' attitude to pupils were an even greater contribution to EMU than the lessons that are taught; the teachers saw the need to respect pupils and to practice an improved sense of justice within their schools. The group also thought it important that principles underpinning EMU must be at the very heart of a common whole school policy. It was agreed that this would be child focussed and take account of the condition of the wider community. It was set out as follows:

... Primary School will try to provide a secure, happy and stimulating environment that will lead to purposeful learning activity. Such an environment will hopefully promote independence and a responsible and caring attitude and thus enrich the development of the whole child. Within the framework the staff will seek to encourage the moral, intellectual, social, physical and emotional development of the child. It is hoped that at the end of a child's education at this school, he/she

will have achieved a level of personal growth of desirable qualities; i.e. be numerate, literate, socially adjusted, morally and spiritually aware and be culturally enhanced. Each child should fulfil his/her potential intellectually, physically, emotionally and socially, having a high level of self-esteem and self-confidence.

School is part of the local community and every effort will be made to participate in local affairs.

The Warnock Report sees education enabling a child to enter the world after formal education is over as an active participant in society, and a responsible contributor to it, capable of achieving as much independence as possible.

The world is not an insular one, a Catholic one or a Protestant one, but a world of mixed religions and cultures. Children must be exposed to the fact that qualities of 'good' and 'bad' are not exclusive to one faith or another and that judgements should not be coloured by race or creed.

It is therefore hoped to promote personal growth and to develop a responsible learner and citizen.

In line with current educational practice pupils will be encouraged to forego all forms of violence - to this end war games and toys are banned from school.

The School will deploy staff and resources to the children's best advantage, paying attention to monitoring work, assessing and record keeping. Special care will be taken with the diagnosis of children's learning difficulties and with their remediation. Staff will receive in-service training to afford the children the benefits of the latest education techniques and innovations ...

The foundations of recent EMU work are now laid in P1-3 through the People who help Us theme. Resources allow for only one day together on the beach in the summer term, but contact builds up from P4 to P7 through other themes and projects. Initial contact begins as a pen-pal letter writing exercise in English; photographs and home telephone numbers are exchanged. Parents are alerted to the possibility of friendships developing. This form of contact is quickly followed up with face-to-face contact at a neutral venue before joint project work is begun across three schools. This involves contact at each other's school and the sharing of resources and expertise. It leads in turn to a residential course where increasingly contentious issues are raised and handled. Follow-up work is thought essential and meetings of children continue to take place in each other's schools and at neutral venues on a regular basis. The principals have agreed to feature each child's EMU experience and contribution to joint work in the transfer reports prepared for the secondary schools in their area (Cranny, 1989).

2.   Five History Departments Together

Established by the ELB, in association with an institution of higher education, a group of history teachers interested in encouraging local history agreed to develop jointly units of study to be phased in for forms 1-3 and to be used over the period of a term as part of an existing programme. Each unit would include an element of pupil contact. The titles of the units were: (i) Peoples of Ireland; (ii) The Ulster Plantation; and (iii) (possibly) The Border Issue.

The material for unit 1 aims *to introduce pupils to the multi-cultural origins of society on the island of Ireland by an examination of the varied settlements throughout the centuries.* It looks at different groups who have settled Ireland from earliest times; pre-history, Celts, Vikings, Normans, various plantations through to more recent immigration and emigrations and asks who these groups were, when and why they came and encourages discussion about the contributions they made and how earlier settlers may have been affected by newcomers.

An introductory exercise involved pupils carrying out a survey and research on the origin of local surnames as a way of opening up the idea that various groups have settled the island throughout history. It also gave some opportunity to show that not all Catholics are descended from Celtic ancestors and not all Protestants from British families. Contact involved both the sharing of work and working together. As a beginning, results of the initial exercise on surnames were exchanged between schools and teachers helped pupils examine the spread of surnames within the community. This was followed by a joint visit to the Ulster American Folk park where pupils worked in mixed groups. The next stage of the contact programme involved a residential trip to Dublin to visit the Viking Exhibition, the National

Museum and, on the way, Newgrange and Monasterboice Abbey before work was undertaken together at Carrickfergus Castle as part of problem-solving exercise on medieval defense arising from a study of the Normans.

The second unit progresses from the first with an indepth look at more controversial issues arising from the local impact of the plantation. It shows how different people can react in different ways to events from the past. Contact included discussion sessions and a residential visit based at the Corrymeela centre involving field work on accessible plantation sites.

Though the group continues to grapple with logistical problems of balance between the sexes and traditions of pupils on future contact work, it feels that taken such a strong lead within their respective schools, there is a danger that the history departments could be left to carry the onus of EMU development in the common curriculum (Smith and Dunn 1990).

3.   One School's Dilemma

In this secondary school there is no agreement as to the impact or value of EMU generally. The school's aims do not specifically refer to EMU but include enabling each pupil to develop *a sense of personal responsibility and confidence so that he/she will play his/ her full part in the life of the school and eventually the community' and encouraging teachers to establish 'the belief that each individual child is important for who he/she is.* It is noticeable in the school that there is lack of communication about and awareness of educational experiences that can be described as EMU. Work is being done in some subjects that can be described as EMU-related and that has the potential to be developed as EMU given some modification of aims and learning experiences. Certain concepts and themes occur in subjects where they might be expected; conflict is a recurring concept in English. Teaching strategies considered necessary for EMU (i.e. discussion and role-play) are more likely to be found in English classes. History and geography include topics based on Ireland/Northern Ireland that could make a contribution towards identity. Differences and similarities between religious denominations are dealt with in RE and problems are raised and discussed through such topics as 'communion' and 'marriage'. RE teachers report however, that pupils know so very little about their tradition.

The school library is reasonably well supplied with books about other cultures but not about those of this island.

Sports fixtures bring pupils into contact with those from other cultural backgrounds. However the competitive element of the game is dominant and there is little time for social contact. Nevertheless, playing for a team does provide opportunities for important EMU experiences of co-operation and interdependence.

Only one contact with another school has been made using financial support from DENI. It involved 10 third-year pupils from each of the two schools doing joint work in technology. An introductory meeting at the ice rink and a concluding visit to a monastery were featured. Pupils were chosen because of their reliable behaviour and ability to benefit from the technology project. While this might be seen as an experimental contact scheme, it did not involve much preparatory work and as teachers also have concerns over legal cover there are no definite plans for a follow-up.

A major innovation in the school has been the introduction of a personal and social development programme. This currently involves first and second-year pupils but it is planned to include pupils within all five years. Much of the content of this programme relates to EMU - self knowledge, respect, respect for others, friendship, dealing with problems.
Indeed, a senior teacher considers that the school is beginning to recognise the need;

- *to develop a policy of EMU within the school*
- *to clarify the nature of EMU among staff*
- *to ensure that EMU is part of all the school's activities*
- *to relate EMU to the specific needs of the school in*
  order to meet the requirement of the common curriculum
- *to develop a structure for inter-school contact.*

(Leckey 1989)

CONCLUDING REMARKS

EMU is not new but the work is only just beginning. Its very existence is a reflection of the dedication of teachers who care about the young and their future and is a measure of success and continued hope. Its continued development within the framework of the Common Curriculum is assured because all teachers care about the education of the young and will find ways of bringing EMU experiences to them. There is more support than ever before and this has been demonstrated as extending to parents (Smith and Dunn 1990; Cuthbert 1990), but EMU for all will still take time.

EMU is not all teachers' expressed priority but it is all teachers' responsibility to collaborate with their colleagues and to contribute to it. This means that all should be aware of their contribution, review that contribution particularly in relation to the statements of attainment targets proposed by ministerial subject groups, be involved in the formulating of policy and the creation of programmes and not the commitment to any EMU co-ordinator appointed by the school. EMU is not easy to teach, or learn, but creative, experimental approaches provide an essential professional development that improves the quality of teaching elsewhere in the curriculum. Continued in-service work and staff development will form an important element of any school EMU development plan. Teacher appraisal (and higher salaries) will help this.

One wonders whether in a further twenty years time parents will use their education vouchers in those schools that have built up the most visible and coherent EMU programme.

CULTURAL HERITAGE

Alexander McEwen

INTRODUCTION

The Cultural Heritage programme is one of six cross-curricular themes introduced to Northern Ireland schools as part of the government's overall approach to educational reforms in the province. Along with the cross-curricular theme of Education for Mutual Understanding, it is meant to bring about a greater appreciation by Protestants and Catholics of their respective cultural, political and historical traditions and in the long term to remove the causes of present community mistrust and animosity. The programme is to be incorporated in the normal curricular subjects so that teachers of history, English, geography science and so on, will be required to include the scheme's objectives in their syllabuses.

The problems that Cultural Heritage programmes attempt to confront can be encapsulated neatly in two alternative analyses of the causes of community conflict and mistrust. The first places the emphasis on schooling and the extent to which it may have contributed to the present 'troubles' through the rigid segregation of Catholic and Protestant children in their respective school systems. This view was clearly and authoritatively expressed by the Cameron Commission of 1972. It recognised a point of view that argued that,

The educational facilities particularly accorded to Catholics tend directly to support a continuance of the division between Protestant and Catholic so as to perpetuate sectarian feelings and antagonisms (Cameron Report 1969 para 151).

The alternative viewpoint places more emphasis on economic, political and cultural factors as having fostered suspicion, mistrust and discrimination. Many have argued that this provides a more likely and more powerful basis for explaining present levels of inter-community tension. The Cameron Report also adverted to this argument,

Much of the evidence of grievance and complaint...was found, as might be expected, to be concentrated upon housing and employment. In both these fields - work and housing - political intervention and discrimination was alleged to be operative (56 para129).

Proponents of the latter analysis would point to such features as patterns of employment that result in different levels and quality of opportunity being presented to Catholics and Protestants. At present, this means that young Catholics are approximately twice as likely to be unemployed as Protestants.

Culturally, the argument would also relate to the perception among Catholics that their 'Irishness' had somehow been devalued and supplanted by an over-representation of British ideas and values as the basis for a Northern Ireland culture. By contrast, Protestants have largely seen 'Irishness' as indistinguishable from republicanism and Catholicism. This perception can be best exemplified in the characteristically hostile attitude of Protestants towards any proposed extension of Irish language teaching to their schools; they would perceive such an activity as deeply politicised and one that would lead to a diminution of the Protestant character of their schools. By contrast, Irish is taught in most Catholic post-primary schools and is strongly associated with the perception of their schools by Catholic teachers and parents as Irish in ethos and orientation. The presence of Irish in most post-primary Catholic secondary schools, therefore, acts both as a defining characteristic of the schools' 'Irishness' and similarly as a powerful outward symbol of the distinctiveness of the Catholic tradition in the face of what, in the past, has been perceived as a hostile 'official' British/Protestant culture.

This chapter will explore the theme's aim of counteracting the process of politicisation of our cultures and the animosity that it engenders through a programme of curricular intervention. The discussion will also raise questions about the effects of wider economic and political issues as formative backgrounds to Catholics' and Protestants' perceptions of their heritages. It seems appropriate to begin an examination of this area with an exploration of the different definitions that people in Northern Ireland have of themselves as alternatively British or Irish.

THE POLITICS OF IDENTITY

The first question raised in the introduction concerns the present nature of the interpretation of their respective cultural heritages by Protestants and Catholics in Northern Ireland. Irish historiography has been the most popular medium for the exploration of this issue ranging from the very broad and comprehensive work of historians such as Lyons (1971) Beckett (1966) and more recently Foster (1989) to highly specific analyses of particularly formative periods such as that given by Fiske (1985). Indeed, it would be difficult to discuss the two communities' approaches to their cultural heritage without some treatment of their respective 'histories' but the main focus here will be on the question of identity as a key element of those 'histories'; they have after all shaped the experiences of the two groups and the major ways in which their traditions have been defined, legitimated and transferred. The argument will concentrate chiefly on schools and employment as the most significant formative arenas for the creation of both individual and community identities.

Firstly, as to the area of employment, the recently formed Fair Employment Commission has one over-riding statistic as its target for change; that Catholics, particularly those in the 16 to 25 age-range, are generally twice as likely to be unemployed as their Protestant counterparts. This is something of an overgeneralization of the Commission's role in scrutinising patterns of recruitment where it very effectively reveals and attempts to counteract the way in which each community tends to 'look after its own' by employing either Protestant or Catholic co-religionists. Unlike its predecessor, the Fair Employment Agency, the Commission now has the power to compel employers, in their recruitment procedures, to be representative of the religious balance in the surrounding community. Discrimination has also been evident with regard to the different types of employment that have, in the past, been 'owned' by the two communities. Higher paid skilled manual workers in manufacturing industries, for instance, are recruited predominantly from the Protestant community; the lower paid, more seasonable and economically vulnerable building and construction workforce has been chiefly Catholic in nature. Identity, both individual and community, cannot but be influenced by these and other sorts of economic realities and the consequently different processes of socialisation experienced by Protestants and Catholics in their families, at work and in the wider community. The resulting attitudes are rarely articulated formally, but they deeply influence perceptions of employment and, more precisely, the opportunity structure available to young people. Ideas of power, control, authority and social equity form the basis of such attitudes and affect perceptions of self and of future employment prospects. More generally, they provide an important reference point for the way each community thinks about, uses, and consolidates its cultural heritage.

The central point here is that these variables produce significant differences between the two main religious groups in Northern Ireland and are likely to affect the characteristics of applicants for jobs and their performance at interviews selection boards. Such attitudes will be manifest in the extent to which people see themselves as 'insiders' or 'outsiders' in the contest involving the major forms of employment and whether they feel themselves to be in control or being controlled in their life situation.

More specifically, such attitudes will probably affect views on the nature of management where 'optimists' could be expected to be more closely in tune with those already managing areas of employment such as manufacturing, the civil service and local government. By contrast, 'pessimists' are liable to settle for a more passive view of their situation and their approach to the existing opportunity structure. The argument here is that a disproportionate number of Catholics, for economic and cultural reasons, will tend to fall within the 'pessimistic' category. Such perceptions have also proved to be a major factor in promoting higher rates of employment for Protestants and higher levels of emigration for Catholics.

In summary, Catholic cultural heritage has been shaped by its relationship to power and to questions of social and economic equity as well as to the status of Northern Ireland as a legitimate and just society. Much of this heritage has, in reality and of necessity, been a form of resistance to what have been seen as forms of Protestant economic and cultural domination. Cathcart (1984) gives a clear account for the way in which Protestant viewpoints became represented, through the BBC, as the ideal or official culture. This, he argues, resulted in the devaluation of forms of entertainment and the censoring of political discussion that was thought to reflect an Irish background. 'Britishness' was the predominant lens through which broadcasting was examined and in a sense 'filtered'. Such an ideology was as damaging, in its way, to Protestants as it was dismissive of Catholic traditions since it gave Protestants a limited and impoverished view of themselves and their cultural heritage as Irish men and women by effectively defining the Irish sources of Protestant culture as strictly limited to the six counties of Northern Ireland. Cathcart also gives an example of this process; he relates how in the late 30's the introduction of music based on Irish folk tradition by the BBC proved controversial. The music was played by a group known as the 'Irish Rhythms' and was seen as belonging to 'foreign culture'. The resulting programme outlived this early opposition and stayed on the air for 30 years and was regularly broadcast in Great Britain, Europe and throughout the world.

EDUCATION AND IDENTITY

Economic imperatives on their own cannot give a sufficient account or explanation of how a community develops a collective view of itself. The way in which such a view is sustained through schooling and leisure pursuits needs also to be examined if a full understanding is to be gained of the nature of the relationship between identity and heritage for both Protestants and Catholics.

Many of those who try to explain Protestants' and Catholics' mistrust and suspicion of each other have devoted considerable attention to certain aspects of the school curriculum such as history, sport and, to some extent, music. In particular, the teaching of history has, in the past, been perceived to generate mutually prejudicial attitudes among very many Protestants and Catholics so that it became a vehicle for republican or loyalist indoctrination. Whatever the truth of this belief it is arguable that recent changes in history teaching have made such an assertion more questionable. There are, however, other less publicly recognised differences in curriculum choices and preferences that are generated by the two identities in Northern Ireland. An example of this was highlighted in research evidence that revealed important differences between Protestant and Catholics boys in their preferences for science subjects: Protestants boys at age 17 were studying these subjects in significantly larger numbers than Catholic boys (McEwen et al 1985). An initial reaction to this finding might be that the culture of Catholic post-primary schools is more humanities based than that of similar Protestant schools. One Catholic headmaster, on receiving the results, expressed his confidence in Catholic education for giving pupils a balanced curriculum. Ostensibly, such a viewpoint reflects traditional thinking about the need for a balanced curriculum but, in this case, it has the unintended effect of deflecting attention from the problem of imbalance that exists between the two communities in terms of their respective intellectual 'property' and the consequences for Catholic students' future employment opportunities. Similar more recent findings indicate that the ideal of balance in the curriculum of Catholic schools unintentionally narrows the employment choices of their pupils with respect to those careers that require a basis of scientific training and knowledge (Osborne 1987). With regard to more general patterns of economic power and cultural primacy, differences between Protestants and Catholics in their uptake of science have been reflected in the differential allocation of jobs and the representation of the two communities' 'histories'.

In more general terms the exercise of power is closely, though not solely, bound up with the control of the opportunities structure where one group, has in the case of Northern Ireland Protestants, achieved, for historical reasons, a degree of monopoly over the better paid and higher status occupations. Such patterns and practices of discrimination are now illegal with respect to employers' recruitment policies, but their effects still mostly exist in the extent to which Catholics' and Protestants' choices are influenced by the over or under-representation of their co-religionists at a particular factory or institution. This is often referred to as the 'chill factor'. These choices are also sustained through the traditional cultural and educational heritages of each community as they are expressed in their schools' academic ambience and their pupils' intellectual preferences. Engineering and technological jobs are a case in point where, in the past, there have been disproportionately few Catholic workers which may, therefore, have resulted in a lack of emphasis on science and technology in Catholic Schools, since the opportunity structure, for wider political and cultural reasons, was weighted against Catholic employment in these types of jobs. In addition, Catholic schools, because of their voluntary status, have to raise 15% of their capital costs (in the past there was a larger percentage to be raised). Science laboratories are necessarily expensive to build and the Catholic authorities have been faced with the task of raising substantial amounts of money to build such facilities from a population that was already economically disadvantaged. Whilst there is no direct evidence available, it would seem reasonable, on this historical basis, to expect some degree of under-provision of science laboratories in the Catholic school system.

In summary, the arguments in this section have set out to situate the question of cultural heritage within the wider contexts of employment, politics and schooling. They are based on the view that, if cross curricular themes such as Cultural Heritage and EMU are to affect any changes in the communities' perceptions, understanding and treatment of each other they must be based on a deeper analysis of their respective Protestant and Catholic identities. It is important to go beyond definitions of cultural identity and heritage that rely solely on historical and educational premises. The view taken here is that each community has developed a particular pattern of meaning systems based on its different cultural, educational and economic experiences. These involve values, inclinations and attitudes towards crucial areas such as power, social and economic equity and ultimately the legitimation of the state's political, legal, moral and economic purposes.

The introduction by the government of a Cultural Heritage programme is evidence in itself that a heterodoxy is needed in the definitions of culture and, particularly, in its treatment in schools of the different and often antipathetic perceptions which Catholics and Protestants have of each other's traditions. The programme represents a timely recognition of the need for an initiative in the whole area of defining cultures on the basis of what the two groups share in their backgrounds. This is a radical shift from former culturally arbitrary approaches to an alternative cultural pattern that challenges what were represented in the past as 'official' or 'ideal' definitions of culture, which were in reality predominately Protestant in orientation. The programme attempts to promote the two heritages as being of equal value and highlights what they share and the large area of overlap between the two traditions. In doing so, it will at least diminish the degree of 'symbolic violence' (Bourdieu 1977) towards Catholic cultural heritage by promoting it through the schools as an integral part of the state's culture and legitimate meaning systems. The converse is equally true with regard to Catholic pupils' appreciation of Protestant traditions as the programme is introduced to their schools and may eventually go someway towards a redefinition of Protestant culture where Unionism and Irishness can co-exist.

In the past, the power structure in Ulster has worked in such a way as to marginalise those who asserted their right to an alternative identity. In some instances this assertion has been used to explain the disadvantages under which Catholics labourers in relation to employment opportunities and their lack of a 'place in the sun'. It has been argued that their insistence on maintaining a separate school system has contributed to Catholic disabilities and former Mister of Home Affairs in the Stormont Government before it was prorogued in 1972 the under-representation of Catholics on the judiciary was the result of the lower competence of Catholic lawyers (Kennedy1971).

Catholics, particularly from manual working backgrounds, did not fully apprehend how the system worked beyond having the feeling that their religion somehow labelled them as being less employable than their Protestant counterparts. This point, however, needs to be set in the context of the overall economic disadvantage of Northern Ireland as a region; a situation which affected both Protestants and Catholics. For Catholics, the difference was that the labelling referred to the religious and cultural qualities of individuals and their community rather than that the system's failure both as an economic unit and in its toleration of widespread patterns of discrimination. Protestants, by contrast, have as a community, although with significant social class differences, experienced a continuity between their cultural processes and heritage, and the meanings and cultural symbols of dominance as they were expressed through their schools.

CULTURAL HERITAGE: FUTURE PROJECTIONS

The likely outcomes of the Cultural Heritage programme will, from the outset, be heavily influenced by the analysis of conflict in Northern Ireland on which the programme's recommendations for action in schools is based. The argument so far has been that only a partial analysis of the sources of prejudice and mistrust has been offered by official bodies such as the Cultural Heritage working group. In its report, the group describe cultural heritage broadly as *humble domestic and farm utensils as well as great literature, art and music.* There is no adequate theory of conflict in such an approach other than a belief that it is a purely cultural phenomenon with its roots in Protestants' and Catholics' ignorance of their respective traditions as expressed, for example, in different choices of literature, music (to some extent) and, in the case of Catholics, participation in Gaelic sports.

The central argument of the present chapter has been that there is another deeper reality which needs to be analysed and confronted if successful inroads are to be made into present levels of misunderstanding and community tension. This other reality concerns the causes of and attitudes towards social and economic inequity as it affects people's future job opportunities as well as the overall economic and cultural standing of their respective communities. Appreciation of each other's traditions and aspirations will only be fully realised when, in addition to the programme's emphasis on cultural prejudices, other more deeply rooted and manifest forms of inequity such as economic and social discrimination are also fully explored.

The strength of the programme lies in its potential to enable Protestants and Catholics to confront some of the sources of their respective misunderstandings and prejudices about each other. Central to this process will be some sort of appreciation and comprehension of what 'Irishness' means to members of both communities. For many Protestants this issue is not apparent since they would not consider themselves to be Irish, preferring to be known solely as British, whilst simultaneously disclaiming any identification with the other national identities of Great Britain. In Northern Ireland, no enduring consensus concerning Irishness has emerged that could provide any real basis for both Protestants and Catholics beginning to feel identified as primarily 'Northern Irish', or Ulster persons. The cultural heritage theme is a welcome attempt to build a basis for each community to understand the other's viewpoints and aspirations.

Another of the programme's strengths lies in the way it deals with the source of this fracture of identity by asking both groups to stop looking only to sources outside the province for characteristics of their communities. While there are individual exceptions, Protestants have looked chiefly to British sources whilst Catholics, sceptical of the moral and political validity of Northern Ireland, have traditionally given primacy to Irish sources in the creation of a common Catholic heritage. This is best exemplified by the different and politically mutually exclusive events which Protestants and Catholics commemorate. These chiefly entail triumphalist celebrations of victories of one group over the other. Such a background provides a bleak landscape for the development of a common cultural heritage. Since the onset of the present 'troubles', the area for compromise between the two groups has grown progressively more narrow under the impact of sectarian murders and larger atrocities such as 'Bloody Sunday' in 1972 or the more recent (1987) Enniskillen bombing. This absence of consensus with regard to identity produces a vacuum in the cultural and political structures of Northern Ireland and leaves only a limited foundation on which social solidarity can be built. The cultural heritage theme can only improve this situation though its emphasis on pupils studying those aspects of their traditions that they share.

The Cultural Heritage programme, therefore, appears to have a formidable task before it. Perhaps its initial handicap lies in the incomplete analysis of the cultural traditions on which the programme is premised. The present argument has been that political and economic discrimination together with 'symbolic violence' in relation to a lack of tolerance of different cultures, have contributed towards two cultural traditions that have few significant points of contact. The programme requires a harder edge with regard to the more material sources of mistrust and prejudice through, for example, looking more closely at the work of the Commission for Racial Equality in Great Britain and similar agencies in America and the European Community. The framers of the programme have already gone some way to providing this international perspective by including, in its objectives, a consideration of the work of the United Nations, Greenpeace and of underprivileged minorities in USA (Hispanics) and Germany (Turks). Additionally, teachers are asked to compare Northern Ireland with other societies with similar problems such as Cyprus and the Basque region.

CONCLUSION : SEGREGATION AND IDENTITY

The fact that there are effectively two quite separate school systems, one Protestant and one Catholic, in Northern Ireland is a further limiting factor in the achievement of the programme's aims. Separateness on the part of the Catholic authorities is justified on the grounds of freedom of religious conscience. Attacks on their insistence in maintaining their schools as distinctively Catholic in character and ethos are perceived by many as a threat to the right to pursue the Catholic religion itself. The fact of separation, however, provides a context in which, through mono-cultural and religious friendships, the hidden curriculum of prejudice and mistrust can frustrate Catholic and also Protestant teachers' ostensible aims of religious and cultural tolerance . Its most striking effect lies in the creation of a group identity among Protestant and Catholic pupils that accentuates the extremes of the opposite community. This relates to perceptions of their political views, discrimination practices in employment, and, not least, their propensity for physical attack through sectarian violence. Such views emerge most strikingly during critical periods where one community feels itself to be particularly threatened. The Ulster Workers' strike of 1974, the republican prisoners' hunger strike of 1982, and the signing of The Anglo-Irish Agreement of 1985 are examples of such occasions.

One of the ways in which the programme attempts to dismantle community based attitudes and prejudices towards the 'other side' is by setting them in an international context. This 'transnational' theme is pursued throughout the programme's guidelines; at age 16, for instance, pupils studying history, should know about 20th century transnational organisations such as the United Nations Organisation, the World health Organisation, and Greenpeace as part of both their history and Cultural Heritage syllabuses. In a similar way, teachers are asked to examine Irish 'migration' in the context of the Dutch in South Africa, penal colonies in Australia and Hispanics in the USA.

To the extent that the programme achieves its aim of promoting greater understanding of each other's community, it is to be welcomed as an antidote to both curricular and street based history. The method involves an enlargement of the frame for understanding to include European and international dimensions of Protestant and Catholic cultural heritages. Such a process, however, is also one of the programme's weaknesses in so far as it lacks a real critical edge in its avoidance or neglect of deeper sources of identity and community tension. These, it has been argued, are to be found in the different experiences of Protestants and Catholics with regard to fundamental life experiences such as employment, their different attitudes towards power and social equity, and, lastly, their perceptions of the legitimacy and justness of the society itself.

THE DEVELOPMENT OF HEALTH EDUCATION

Samuel McGuffin

INTRODUCTION

Of the six cross-curricular themes in education 'Health Education' has been on the agenda for longer than most of the other elements. In 1975 the Northern Ireland Schools Curriculum Committee (NISCC) supported the first research into health education in schools (McGuffin, 1976) and the trials of the first draft teaching materials for primary schools (Houlton et al, 1976). Consequently when the Minister established his Working Group in January 1989 he was able to appoint several members who had taught and supported Health Education programmes in schools over a fairly long period and some who had been involved in writing materials for schools.

The remit of the Working Group was to make recommendations on the content of Health Education so as to ensure that all essential areas of learning, experience and understanding were adequately covered and on how the content was to be incorporated into the various compulsory subjects and reinforced through the other curricular subjects (DENI 1989a). Account was to be taken of relevant materials already produced including the NICED Primary guidelines : Health & Social Education (1983) and the NICED (1989) guideline : Health Education within the Curriculum 5-19. Although the remit of the group did not refer to consultation with other groups, the Information Technology group was required to contribute to the work of the other cross-curricular working parties by liaising with the chairmen (DENI 1989b). One of the outcomes of the meetings of chairpersons was an agreement on terminology for use in relation to cross-curricular themes to avoid confusion with terms used for subjects. Whereas sub-divisions of subjects were termed profile components each of which had a number of attainment targets, it was agreed that, where necessary, cross-curricular themes would be divided into sub-themes and these into objectives. In place of programmes of study, the cross-curricular themes would have content defined for each objective. Statements of attainment would be prepared for each theme but specific levels would not be associated with these, in order to enable subject working groups to allocate each statement to the level most appropriate in terms of its own programme of study.

The context in which the Health Education group undertook its work reflected over a decade of development in Health Education in both primary and secondary schools in the province. The work of a number of national projects, including the *Schools Health Education 5-13* (HEC, undated) and *13-16* (later 13-18) (SC/HEC, 1980), the *HEC : My Body*, (HEC, 1983), *Natural Nashers* (HEC, 1986) and *Active Tutorial Work* (Baldwin & Wells, 1979-81) projects, and *Skills for Adolescence* (TACADE et al, 1986) and the locally produced *AIDS awareness package* (EHSSB/NICED, 1988) had been disseminated in the province. A number of teachers were being trained to act as coordinators of Health Education programmes in schools and many more were trained to use the materials in their own classes. More recently the Health related fitness programme (Irvine, 1988) had been introduced into schools. However, the uptake of these materials has not been uniform across the province, nor indeed within individual schools, as reflected in the report of the DENI Inspectorate (DENI 1990).

The major issues in the development of Health Education have centred around

a definition
the relation of health education to personal and social education
the best model for use in schools
its aims and objectives
the content of syllabuses
the organisation in schools
the mode of delivery in the classroom
its assessment and evaluation

DEFINITION OF HEALTH EDUCATION

Any definition of Health Education will depend on the concept of health on which it is based. Definitions of health vary from the rather the very wide. Dictionaries define health as 'soundness of freedom from disease'. This narrow concept has been more fully uescribed as free of diseases, fit and able to take an active part in games and social activities, not getting tired too quickly or easily, being less vulnerable to colds and infections. (Pring 1984, 130).

In 1984 the World Health Organisation expanded its earlier definition of health to read *not merely the absence of disease but a state of complete mental, physical and social well-being* (UHO, 1984). This wider concept was expressed in the primary school publication All about me as *health embraces not only physical health and hygiene but also emotional and social facets of human life* (SCHEP, 1977).

The first type of definition, which is negative in tone, represents what has been called the 'medical' model of health, with the second, which is positive, being the 'social' model or more correctly the 'wholeness' model. If any one of the three elements, social, mental or physical well being is absent, good health is absent (SC/HEC, 1980 p 112). Our health, whichever concept is accepted, is influenced by a combination of factors, some within our own control and others in the environment over which an individual has no control. In this sense health is not apolitical, it is not divorced from social, environmental and economic contexts (Burrage 1987).

As there is not an easily accessible positive index of the health of a nation, the mortality rates provide the best available data. At the turn of the century, of the approximately 17 deaths per thousand of the population, 7 (41%) were due to infectious diseases, whereas recent figures indicate that of the 12.5 deaths per thousand only 1 (18%) was so caused. The most common causes of death have changed from tuberculosis, scarlet fever, whooping cough and diphtheria to heart disease, cancer and cerebrovascular disease. As far as the school age population is concerned the two most common causes of death currently are accidents and cancer. (extracted from data in McKeown & Lowe 1979; OPCS 1979).

The idea that Health Education would assist in transmitting the knowledge that enabled young people to remain healthy arose naturally from the medical model of health (Pring 1984, 130). There is evidence, however, that 'telling the facts' approach has had very limited effect on children's health behaviour (DES 1977) but also evidence of an association, not necessarily causal, between health knowledge and behaviour in school leavers (McGuffin 1983). That giving the facts is insufficient is reflected in definitions of Health Education based on the social or wholeness model of health. The Working Paper (Schools Council 1976 13) accepted the definition that Health Education is the totality of experience from which individuals learn behaviours related to their health and this was refined in the Schools Council 5-13 Project as including those planned experiences which will benefit the physical, emotional and social lives of children (SCHEP 1977). To achieve these ends the main concern of Health Education is not with knowledge and understanding but with decision-making, attitudes, values and social skills. This view was reflected in the decision of the Northern Ireland Certificate of Secondary Education (NICSE) Board to change the title of its examination in Health Education to Human Biology as from 1984 without any substantial change of syllabus content (NICSE 1981, 1982). The wider point of view is taken by the HEC : My Body Project (HEC, 1983) which stated that the aim of Health Education should be to increase children's ability to make choices about the things that affect their health. Consequently Health Education is seen as omnipretentious, to lay claim not only to relatively factual areas in biology and home economics but also to venture into 'soft' areas of values and feelings. (Tones 1987 4). In particular, the boundaries between what is termed Health Education and the recently developing area called personal and social education are extremely blurred. This situation was reflected in the NICED (1983) Primary Guidelines which was entitled *Health and Social Education* and which did not define its field but was content to quote a few prominent authorities in an attempt to clarify its meaning (NICED, 1983 p 1-2). Neither did the NICED (1989) guideline Health Education within the curriculum 5-19, offer a definition but contented itself with an introduction which discussed the philosophy of Health Education (pp 1-2). With these precedents the Working Group in its report did not include a definition but as the other five cross-curricular working groups each offered a definition of its field, NICC requested a definition for Health Education in order to facilitate a uniform presentation in its report. The definition provided was that Health Education is any combination of learning opportunities designed to bring about behaviour which is conducive to good health (NICC 1989, 18).

THE RELATION OF HEALTH EDUCATION TO PERSONAL AND SOCIAL EDUCATION

Health Education is frequently confused with Personal and Social education. A major problem is to decide where one ends and the other begins. Neither the consultation document (DENI 1988a) nor the White Paper (DENI 1988b) had any reference to personal and social education or the pastoral curriculum, although the former referred to the curriculum containing all the essential elements to enable pupils to develop to their full potential and make their contribution to society, whether in their chosen career, personal and family life or social activities (para 4). As the major causes of ill-health are diseases which to a large degree result from patterns of life-style rather than from environmental circumstances, the importance of the affective domain involving attitudes, values and decision-making has become paramount. This is the aspect of education primarily associated with Personal and Social Education (PSE).

In PSE three inter-related ideas are involved, namely the 'health career', personal responsibility for one's own health and self-concept. The notion of a 'health career' is based on the belief that the health behaviour of individuals has a history of development, involving knowledge, values, beliefs, attitudes, expectations and experiences, which begins at a very early age. It is important to help pupils accept that their health is largely a personal responsibility. Behaviour, in many circumstances, is influenced by the images they have of themselves - the self-concept (Williams & Williams 1981). Without a guarantee of provision for personal and social education it was therefore imperative that the content of Health Education be so defined as to include the affective domain. Subsequently many respondents to the Working Party report saw aspects of Health Education as part of the pastoral curriculum and there was overwhelming support for the inclusion of a unit of work on Health

Education in the pastoral curriculum (NICC 1989 7). Following this publication NICC announced plans to issue non-statutory guidance on the place of the pastoral curriculum within the whole curriculum of the school.

A MODEL OF HEALTH EDUCATION

A number of models, some variously described, of Health Education have been proposed. The medical, or preventive medical model has also been called the knowledge-attitude-behaviour model. It is based on the idea that knowledge about a subject leads to a change in attitude and consequently in behaviour. It is teacher-directed and implicitly or explicitly contains a degree of victim blaming. (SSCR 1987 10). The aim of personal development or self-empowerment model is to produce greater self-awareness and an attitude of personal responsibility for health. It uses problem-solving exercises, role play and discussion of different life-styles and the influence of culture and society upon health. (SSCR 1987 11). The radical or environmental/political health model seeks to focus on the root cause of ill health which it is claimed lies in the social structure of nations and communities. Having been made aware of the social origins of ill health people should be persuaded into collective action to create health promoting environments (Freudenberg 1981). A fourth model, the educational model, as described by Tones (1987) combines to a fair degree the first two models already described. It acknowledges that information about health issues alone is insufficient to bring about behaviour change. It considers the primary role of Health Education is to facilitate decision-making irrespective of the nature of the decision, but acknowledges that promoting informed decision-making is a goal which is emotionally satisfying but difficult to achieve in practice. It is conceded that like the model this is philosophically problematical, because of the illusory nature of genuine free choice which is offered as such a worthwhile goal.

The model adopted in the report was that described in the NICED (1989) guideline (p 1-2) which combined the knowledge-attitude-behaviour, personal development and environmental/political models. It focused on the increasing autonomy of the individual, acknowledging that awareness, knowledge and understanding of health issues can be acquired not only by direct information but also by collecting local and national data and by considering differences in trends that may be shown by the data in the context of the prevailing cultural, social and political climate. Health issues provide a context for the development of personal skills such as observing, searching for information, thinking, listening, analysing, talking and questioning and also of the inter-personal skills of discussing, sharing, co-operating, trusting and mutual respect. Opportunities can be provided, at least to some degree in school, for realistic decision-making, in which context care has to be taken to ensure that the hidden curriculum of the school does not expose pupils to conflicting messages. In these ways the autonomy of the individual can be increased, self-esteem enhanced and self-improvement extended.

THE AIMS OF HEALTH EDUCATION

Arising from the adoption of the model as described above, the aims for Health Education as set out in the Appendix to the NICED (1989, 63) guidelines were accepted. They were deliberately ordered to emphasise the importance of the affective domain. Those referring to achievement of potential, improvement of self-knowledge and self-esteem, positive attitudes to health, a sense of responsibility for health and a healthy life-style were placed first in the list. The acquisition of skills in relation to decision-making, and the management of situations of stress in relation to health followed and the final aim was to provide pupils with the skills to understand and interpret the relevant knowledge which would be given as the essential base for a comprehensive Health Education programme.

THE OBJECTIVES OF HEALTH EDUCATION

In order to structure a Health Education programme which would achieve the aims set out above, a three-part division of the cross-curricular theme was proposed. This identified the personal development, and the social development of the individual and the environmental context in which the individual lived as the essential features. This pattern followed very closely the three foundation stones, namely, looking after self, relationships and community/environment, identified by Williams (1987 71).

For each of the three sub-themes a set of objectives was devised. In most cases the first part of the statement of the objective involved the affective domain and this was followed by a reference to the relevant cognitive material. For example, the objective in relation to nutrition read : Pupils should be able to make responsible decisions about their diet. They should know and understand the contribution of food to growth, energy and health. (DENI 1989a, 4-5)

Four aspects of personal development were identified, namely, physical and emotional growth, physical fitness, nutrition and the problems associated with potentially harmful substances. Three dimensions of relationships, namely, those within the family, with peers, and with others within a widening community, constituted the objectives in relation to social development. It was recognised that personal safety in and responsibility for maintaining and improving the physical environment were essential features of the third sub-theme.

THE CONTENT OF HEALTH EDUCATION SYLLABUSES

The major part of the remit of the Minister's Working Group was to detail the content of Health Education to ensure that all essential areas of learning, experience and understanding were adequately covered. The NCC Consultation Report on Science (NCC 1988) was available to the group who used the relevant parts of the recommended programmes of study and statements of attainment contained therein as an initial basis for considering the content of sub-theme 1 : personal development, In particular the attainment targets entitled *Processes of life, Genetics and Evolution* were found especially appropriate while that entitled *Human Influences on the Earth* was helpful in relation to the sub-theme on the environment. Additional material for personal development, physical and emotional, together with much basic material in relation to social development was available in the publications of the Home and Family 8-13 Project (Schools Council 1979 10-15, 50-55). This was set out in detail for three stages of development namely firstly; the early stage of concrete thinking, secondly; the later stage thereof and thirdly; the early stage of abstract thinking. When the content had been drafted in reasonably developmental sequence, it was divided into the four key stages as prescribed in the White Paper, although for aspects of social development the two key stages in the secondary sector which coincide with the period of adolescence were considered together as young people reach various stages of development at different ages.

ORGANISATION IN SCHOOLS

The remit of the Working Group was confined to specifying the content of Health Education. Although the Group was not required to make recommendations on either the organisation of Health Education in schools or its mode of delivery in the classroom, it was concerned that the good practice which had been established over a decade in many schools should become the norm in all schools. Accordingly it adopted the only method which seemed appropriate by expressing three concerns in its letter to the Minister which accompanied the report (DENI 1989a). It drew attention to the importance of the pastoral component of the curriculum, to the need for co-ordination of Health Education throughout the school and to the need for in-service training for all teachers in the techniques appropriate to learning in the affective domain. These points reflected the identification in recent years of a number of issues relating to organisation of Health Education in schools, namely, the importance of planning and co-ordination, the significance of the hidden curriculum and the changing concept of the role of the school to that of a 'health promoting' school.

In the primary sector, attention had been drawn to the need for a carefully planned spiral curriculum to ensure that all aspects of Health Education were adequately covered in a progressive sequence appropriate to the maturity and needs of the pupils without unnecessary repetition of the same material. To ensure this the identification of a teacher to oversee the plan, to co-ordinate resources and to support his/her colleagues was seen to be highly desirable (HEC undated).

In the secondary sector, the situation is much more complex owing to the number of departments which make a contribution to Health Education, to the wide range of needs of young people as they develop through adolescence, and to the pressure of public examination requirements. The importance of the role of a Health Education team has been recognised. Its role includes the co-ordination of the content, timing and approach of different subjects to the various themes of Health Education and the resolution of problems arising from the choice of subjects at 13 or 14 which may lead to either considerable overlap and repetition or almost complete neglect of certain essential aspects of health. In due course when the requirements of the new curriculum apply to years 11 and 12, it is anticipated that this problem will decrease as all pupils will be required to study a much wider range of subjects than is the current practice (NI Office 1989).

In recent years the importance of the pastoral role of the class or form teacher has been increasingly recognised and the link between the work of personal and social development directly involved in that role with the more normal Health Education input of subjects has been identified (Baldwin & Wells 1979-81 ; TACADE et al 1986).

The hidden curriculum is taken to include the caring relationships established in the school, the example set by teachers, the relationships developed between home and school and the physical environment and facilities of the school (Young 1990). The report (DENI 1989a) made the point that it is essential, whether in relation to discipline, the condition of toilet and changing facilities, the food available in the tuckshop or dining hall or the general attitude to safety, that there is no conflict with the concepts, principles and presentation of Health Education in the classroom (p 4).

The concept of the health promoting school has developed from the more general approach of health promotion in the community (SHEG, 1986). In the content of the aim of the *UHO Health for all by 2000* the role of the school has been examined (UHO 1987) and the European Community has issued guidelines for schools (EC 1988). Health promotion seeks not only to influence individual choices but to foster environmental change through legal, fiscal, economic and political action - to make 'the healthy choice the easy choice' (Tones 1987, 39). Many of the aspects included in the consideration of the hidden curriculum are also relevant, in particular, relations between the school and the local community, especially in relation to parental involvement and co-operation and the use of the school health services. It is important that the screening and disease prevention services are integrated into the school system and seen to contribute significantly to the practical application of the learning in school.

THE MODE OF DELIVERY IN THE CLASSROOM

The Working Party report (DENI 1989a, 6) recognised that the formulation of attitudes, and the clarification of values and the resulting development of behaviour patterns involved the exercise of a range of personal and social skills. The development of these skills requires sufficient time and an appropriate learning environment. It was realised that not all teachers are at present trained to use the variety of techniques appropriate to work in the affective domain (Rice, 1981) and that not all teaching spaces provide an appropriate environment. The NICED guideline (NICED, 1989) devotes a chapter to approaches to Health Education (p 46-49) and lists a range of active learning strategies ranging from brain-storming and buzz groups through drama and role play to stand point taking and verbal tennis. It also explains how the traditional arrangement in classrooms can be modified to provide a more congenial and encouraging atmosphere for activities which involve working and discussion in groups.

EVALUATION AND ASSESSMENT

Two aspects of accountability in Health Education have been distinguished by the terms evaluation and assessment. Evaluation is usually taken to imply the investigation of the value and success of a programme. More recently the term effectiveness has been introduced to replace evaluation and also to highlight the difference between effectiveness in a qualitative sense and efficiency which measures the extent to which a Health Education intervention has achieved a given outcome compared with some alternative intervention (Tones et al 1990, x). For example, the evaluation of the Northern Ireland AIDS teaching pack assessed to what extent its objectives had been achieved but there was no other intervention for comparison (Cullen & McGuffin, 1989). Evaluation involves addressing a number of questions about a programme of Health Education such as:

were the aims and objectives appropriate?
how far were the aims and objectives achieved?
were the teaching methods appropriate?
were the classroom facilities adequate?
were adequate resources and materials available?

Under the new Education Reform Order this evaluation will be the responsibility of the Inspectorate of DENI.

As Health Education involves both the cognitive and affective domains, the assessment of the progress of individual pupils requires a range of approaches. In the cognitive domain an objective scheme, involving a linear progression of skills would be appropriate. Such skills would include knowledge of facts, interpretation and critical evaluation of data or evidence and problem solving abilities. The Working Party identified such aspects of each of the objectives (DENI 1989, 8-19). Subsequently the subject working parties in English, Mathematics and Science considered these and incorporated them in their statements of attainment as appropriate. In particular, many of these statements appear in the Science Consultation report under attainments targets 5 : The variety of life, : 6 Processes of life and 7 : Genetics and evolution (NICC 1990, 42-47). The progress of pupils in these attainment targets will be reported at the end of the four key stages - at ages 8, 11, 14 and 16 -in terms of which of the ten levels the pupil has achieved.

The assessment in the affective domain presents problems of a different dimension. Many aspects, such as attitudes, values and elements of behaviour are extremely difficult to measure reliably (APU 1981). Various approaches such as the use of criterion-referencing of skills, self-assessment and pupil profiling have been proposed (SSCR 1987, 49-56 ; SC/HEC 1980, 169-177 ; Broadfoot 1989, 290-299). Many teachers doubt whether it is right that such aspects of a young person should be assessed and reported upon (Williams, 1987, 63). White the Working Party accepted that formal testing was not appropriate, it considered that positive achievement in certain activities merited recording and recommended that this be included in the pupil's personal record of achievement. (DENI, 1989a, 21).

CONCLUSION

Unlike schools in England and Wales where as yet there is no legislative requirement in respect of Health Education, Northern Ireland schools are required as from September 1990 to include Health Education as a cross-curricular theme delivered mainly through subjects. The Working Party report to the Minister was based on the experience gained over more than a decade, during which many schools had incorporated Health Education into their curriculum and many teachers had been trained either as co-ordinators and/or in active learning methods. However, in spite of the existence of an up-to-date guideline (NICED 1989) and high quality materials produced by many projects, there is considerable apprehension about the successful implementation of Health Education in all schools for all pupils unless steps are taken to ensure proper planning and co-ordination and all teachers are convinced of its value and are adequately prepared to adopt appropriate teaching approaches.

INFORMATION TECHNOLOGY IN THE CURRICULUM

John Gardner

THE CHALLENGE OF THE COMMON CURRICULUM

The implementation of the common curriculum is steadily gathering momentum. Teachers and pupils are now confronting the complexities of an educational innovation that, compared to others in the past, has that extra dimension of being enshrined in statute. The curriculum has become a highly structured entity, with old and new concepts worked into a matrix of pupil performance measures and assessment procedures.

The commonly held view that the attainment targets are stiflingly prescriptive is somewhat modified when the more flexible programmes of study are examined. After all is said and done we retain the flexibility to design and organize our classroom activities as we see fit. The school timetable has become more constrained but the subject matter that we teach has in reality suffered no more than a reorganization, some cuts here, some additions there. We are still endeavouring to impart more or less the same set of skills, knowledge and understanding to our charges.

The new curriculum may have set new priorities for defining the content of our teaching but the main challenge for many of us lies outside our subject knowledge base. That challenge relates to the manner in which we teach and to the manner in which our pupils learn. Even in the compartmentalized (subject-based) environment of secondary level education, a variety of influences will cause us to undertake more collaborative teaching across the subject boundaries and will place greater emphasis on pupils taking a more active role in their learning, inside and outside the classroom. One of the main agents in this change will be the implementation of the cross-curricular themes.

CROSS CURRICULAR THEMES

Cross-curricularity is not a simple concept. If we consider a cross-curricular approach to, say, Health Education we find that it is not simply a case of defining the knowledge, skills and understanding associated with it, dividing these into their component parts and then allocating them to various subjects as the nominated vehicles for teaching them. This cannot be the case - and the reason is embodied in the saying: 'the sum of the parts does not make a whole'. Certainly there are elements of any educational theme that can be defined as a body of knowledge, skills or understanding that needs to be developed and there will be some subjects more appropriate as the teaching (or learning) vehicles than others. In the case of health education, it might be argued that science, for example, would be able to offer explanations for our pursuit of hygiene while PE might be the subject to provide for its practice.

Ownership of such components is not, however, the issue. Cross-curricularity goes deeper than this. Something which is recognised as being of cross-curricular status will be viewed as fundamental to a pupil's development. It will therefore find meaningful expression in many different subject contexts. It is inevitable that there will be overlap and repetition but this is entirely acceptable while the activities are meaningful and purposeful in the contexts in which they arise. There is an important inference here that a feature of the cross-curricularity of a subject is that it should not necessarily be taught in a contrived way.

Some skills may need to be deliberately taught, and indeed some knowledge may need to be deliberately imparted but often the aims of a cross-curricular theme may be better served by exploiting their natural emergence in a lesson, enabling pupils to assimilate them in a meaningful context. This does not mean we should do nothing but wait for them to emerge but it does mean we should take our opportunities to develop cross-curricular objectives whenever we can. Similar opportunities may thus arise in several subjects (overlap and repetition) and this will have the added impact of there being several distinct contexts in which the same message or activity has meaning.

Cross-curricularity is not a new concept - we have always had instances in our teaching, in all subjects, of examining issues that go beyond a subject's strict knowledge base or examination syllabus. Perhaps in most cases until now, the cross-curricularity of the pupils' work has come about more by accident than design. The new curricular approaches aim to change this.

Consider, for example, the planning of a school trip to Brussels. If the pupils were to become involved they could examine a variety of aspects related to the project, for example:

Where is Brussels? How far away is it? How do you get to it from Northern Ireland ? Who provides the transport and how much do they charge? What is the cheapest method of getting to it? Is this the quickest? Why not? Where can you stay in Brussels? What should you want to visit or look out for? What is Belgium famous for? What has been its recent history? What kind of industries does it have? What languages are spoken there? What are its neighbouring countries? How does Belgium run its governmental affairs?

Clearly such a project would benefit from collaboration across a number of subject boundaries, most notably geography, mathematics, history, languages and English. Many activities need to be undertaken: letters to be written, telephone calls to be made, costs to be compared, information to be found, locations and itineraries to be identified and planned, money to be raised, tickets to be booked and doubtless many more. All in all a breadth of learning opportunity and a wealth of learning outcomes.

In some respects the cross-curricular themes have tried to focus on the kinds of things that can feature in almost any class. Opportunities, for example, can arise at any time in any class for the treatment of such issues as job prospects (careers education), personal and domestic finances (Economic Awareness), how other people do things (Education for Mutual Understanding / Cultural Heritage), healthy or unhealthy practices (health education) or the use of new technologies in everyday life (Information Technology).

Some of these theme topics will be more appropriate in some subjects but the aim of the common curriculum is that the breadth of experiences that pupils are exposed to in their compulsory education should deliver the full range of knowledge, skills and understanding embodied in each cross-curricular theme.

IT AS A CROSS CURRICULAR THEME

Since 1981, the government and the main body of IT educationalists have been trying to persuade schools to see to it that our pupils leave school with a competence in IT that will enable them to adapt to and indeed exploit the world's growing dependence on IT. Millions of pounds have been spent in providing schools with the necessary equipment but the fact is that much of this investment has so far benefitted only a small number of pupils - those pupils who elected to take the burgeoning subject of computer studies at 'O' level and GCSE. In most schools those who did not elect to do it (and this included a majority proportion of girls) had little opportunity either as juniors or indeed as 'A' level seniors, to receive the exposure the government intended and the educationalists wanted. Something had to give and in the end it was computer studies.

Not even mentioned in *The Way Forward* the writing was on the wall for computer studies as schools came to terms with a timetable overburdened with other curricular requirements. Information technology was identified as a cross-curricular theme, and a competence in its processes was considered a fundamental objective of every pupil's compulsory education. Each subject now has a responsibility to exploit opportunities for IT usage - where and when it is meaningful and practical. In this manner pupils should experience a breadth of IT usage and therefore develop their knowledge, skills and understanding from primary key stage 1 right through to the completion of their secondary key stage 4.

IT COMPETENCE

It's all very well to say that compulsory education should foster a pupil's IT competence but the first question that leaps to anyone's mind is 'What is IT competence?' Nothing is ever simple of course and the answer will be different depending on who is asked. In essence, however, certain principles can be identified.

Firstly, there is the knowledge base. Pupils will need to know about the types of IT tools that exist. They will need to know that the basic IT tools are word processors, databases and spreadsheets and they will need some level of familiarity with more specialized tools for activities such as desk top publishing and electronic communication. They should appreciate that computers can store vast amounts of information, can carry out complex calculations if need be, can manipulate all of this information and can enable us to structure and present the information for communicating to others. They also need to appreciate that many of these functions can be automated and can be integrated and merged at our behest.

Secondly, pupils need to develop IT skills. They should be confident and competent with a range of IT tools and be able to adapt to new or unfamiliar variants of the same tool type. They need to be able to analyse their needs in any context and be able to select appropriate IT tools for their purposes.

Bound in with the need to accumulate knowledge and to develop skills, pupils will also need to understand IT. In order for pupils to be able to adapt to new or unfamiliar variants of the common tools, they will need a basic understanding of the generic features and uses of each tool. They will need to understand not only that any word processor will offer facilities for editing and presenting texts, any database will offer facilities for interrogating collections of information according to selection criteria and any spreadsheet will offer facilities for applying mathematical processes to collections of numbers. Just as any two cars might have different means of engaging gears, any two word processors will have different means of moving a paragraph. If the pupils are technically confident (i.e. used to computers) this level of understanding will enable them to adapt quickly to new tools.

An extension of the pursuit of this technical understanding is the need for pupils to understand how IT affects everyday life - inside and more particularly outside the school. This is crucial to the pupils being able to exploit the IT developments of today and tomorrow and yet, before we can provide an environment that is sufficiently rich in IT experience for our pupils, we must first of all be conversant with the technology and its techniques, ourselves. So what do we need to know about IT and its applications?

WORD PROCESSORS, DATABASES AND SPREADSHEETS

The baseline for our own, indeed anybody's, competence must be word processing. A word processor is an IT tool that enables us to manipulate text on the screen of a computer and then, when we are satisfied with it, to print it out on paper. It removes the need to correct typescript manually (erasers, masking fluid and so on) and allows us to edit, amend and restructure the text, and even check spellings, easily and quickly. Typing skills are relativey unimportant in the process; most of us will forever type with one or two fingers while only a small number will ever approach the skill and proficiency of a copy typist. With the variety of resources that there is in schools, some may have to master procedures that are overly technical (e.g. for older machines such as the BBC computer and the word processor View), while others may have the push button 'friendliness' of the Apple Macintosh. There is no doubt that the diversity of provision, with its associated diversity of 'user-friendliness', is a major barrier to widespread and easy take-up of the techniques by teachers.

The use of databases is equally important but perhaps less amenable than word processing to someone seeking a baseline IT competence. Unlike word processing, with its links to the widely understood activities of typing, databases are not so easily conceptualized and therefore are not so readily taken up by teachers. But are they so far from a teacher's familiar working base? In essence a database is a collection of information that, because it is structured, is easily searched in response to information requests. Any collection of structured information is a database, be it a set of class marks in the Christmas test, a card file of pupil addresses or a filing cabinet drawer of laboratory resource suppliers. In all such collections some form of alphabetical or numerical order is imposed to provide the structure. A computer database is no different - the information is ordered and structured and the searching is carried out electronically according to the criteria that the requested information will satisfy. As with word processors, it is not the conceptual basis of database usage that ultimately confounds us, it is the lack of familiarity with computers and the all too frequently ill-thought out and cumbersome, not to say occasionally irrational, techniques for using their database facilities.

The third element of the IT baseline trio, and the one with perhaps the most restricted uptake, is the spreadsheet. Although it is basically a simple device for carrying out calculations and combinations of calculations, few teachers outside mathematics, and until recently only a relative few within those ranks, would actually be proficient and purposeful users of spreadsheets. They are in fact excellent tools for monitoring accounts (e.g. the day-to-day tuck shop sales or the results of the school's third-world fund raising activities) and for exploring mathematical equations using 'charting'

Surveys often arise from pupil projects or field work, most frequently in mathematics, science and geography. In most cases pupils gather the data through some measurement mechanism e.g.:

observation: number of cars passing the school gate;
measurement: heights of first formers;
questionnaire: the spending patterns of fourth formers .

They would then enter their data into a spreadsheet to carry out simple operations such as totals or more complex statistical operations such as standard deviation analysis. Frequently they will use their data projectively i.e. they will change one element of their data to see the type of effect this has on other related items. For example if the tuck shop was to increase its price for potato crisps, say one penny, what increase in income could be expected over the next month? If the increase in price caused a ten percent decrease in sales what then would be the effect?

Such calculations, spread over months and even years of data, are carried out almost instantaneously by a spreadsheet. In effect the pupils' data constitute a 'model' of the daily spending patterns in the school tuck shop and as such may be used to predict the effects of changes in the tuck shop's pricing strategies. This type of usage is termed 'modelling' and is a simple introduction to the way in which much corporate and public planning is conducted, with the assistance of powerful IT tools, in the world today.

There seems little doubt that as a body of people, teachers have a professional and personal interest in developing their competence to face the challenges of IT in education. What is in doubt is the best way to achieve this. There are many approaches. Local authorities and subject associations continue to sponsor in-service courses. Field officers with practical experience of the techniques are visiting schools. Cluster groups are providing peer support and individuals are pursuing their development through night classes and so on. Schools themselves are providing study days and are appointing IT co-ordinators in an endeavour to stimulate a school-based and collective approach to the problems.

All of these approaches have their merits but in the end it comes to each one of us being able, by whatever means, to meet the challenge of providing a meaningful IT dimension to the learning opportunities that our pupils experience in our classes. And again, the emphasis is on 'meaningful'. It always has been, and always will be, counter-productive to use inappropriate approaches or over-contrived contexts in the delivery of our teaching and this is no less true for our selection of IT activities. If it cannot be taught as well or better using IT there should be no pressing obligation or justification for using it.

IT IN THE CURRICULUM

Logic demands that the basic IT competence we require of pupils should be part and parcel of our repertoire also. Everyone should be at home with word processors and databases - not necessarily highly skilled in all of their intricacies but certainly capable of making minimal and routine use of them. A degree of competence with spreadsheets should be a feature of all teachers who have any numerate dimension to their work e.g. mathematics, science, geography and technology while all teachers should have a conceptual grasp, if not a working knowledge, of the role that spreadsheets can play.

The curriculum documentation is the starting place. The programmes of study give general guidance on the integration of cross-curricular themes in, normal class work. Taking English as an example, the programme of study for key stage 2 includes the advice:

In the context of their work in English, pupils should understand the role of IT in the community and have opportunities to develop competence in its use for communication and information handling:

by understanding that the word processor can be used to enable the restructuring and refining of written work ...

and for key stage 3:

... use IT to communicate electronically with audiences beyond the school..

Further examples of possible IT usage in English lessons are provided as 'non statutory' illustration of the attainment targets:

Find out about space travel from suitable picture books, magazines, study packs and computer programs.

Design the front page of a magazine using DTP (Desk Top Publishing).

Use a computer database to access information for a project on local studies.

Integrate manuscript, computer processed text, artwork, computer graphics, into a foyer wall display on the theme of 'poverty' for school charity week.

Vary the choice of words, amend sentence structure and paragraphing, move blocks of text (using a word processor if available).

The attainment target sections of the curriculum documents give more precise indications of attainment levels in IT which pupils should progress through in their work. In the tables below, I have collated the majority of the attainment level statements that explicitly involve IT, for the core subjects of science, mathematics and English. In some cases where the appropriate IT tool is not detailed, I have appended, in italics, my suggestions for which type of tool(s) would need to be used.

Mathematics (level 5 upwards)

A2	6b	*use spreadsheets to investigate the feasibility of a simple business project;*
A3	7b	*generate various types of graphs on a computer or calculator and interpret them; (spreadsheets)*
S1	6c	*use computers to generate and transform 2-d shapes; (LOGO)*
S2	6c	*devise instructions for a computer to produce desired shapes and paths; (LOGO)*
Dl	Sc	*insert and interrogate data in a computer database and draw valid conclusions; (databases)*
D2	9a	*present a set of complex data in simplified form, using a variety of diagrams, graphs and computer statistical packages. (spreadsheets)*

English (level 3 upwards)

Writing

3c.5	*use a word processor where appropriate;*
4a.3	*write legibly and fluently in a connected style which accords with school policy, composing where appropriate on computer screen; (word processors)*
Sc	*show independence in planning, revising and re-drafting some writing in manuscript or on computer screen; (wordprocessors)*
6c	*show independence and competence in handling the preparation*

> *And revision of written work, either on paper or on computer screen; (word processors)*

6h *present the writing appropriately, clearly and attractively for the intended readership, using available presentational devices. (word processors)*

Science (level 5 upwards)

3: IT in Science design and use a simple data collection sheet; (databases)

Sb *identify, select and use appropriate communication tools for different tasks;*

6a *use a sensor to detect changes in physical environment and measure physical quantities over a period of time; (control systems)*

6b *use suitable software to redesign or model a given scientific process involving several variables and the relationship between them; (spreadsheets)*

7a *use IT devices to monitor and control experiments; (control systems)*

8a *prepare and present findings in the form of reports which incorporate tables, graphs, diagrams and text and involve the selection and use of appropriate IT systems; (integrated word processor, database, spreadsheet and drawing packages)*

9a *locate and use appropriate sources to gather data in the context of a complete scientific investigation; (control systems, databases)*

9b *design a database using an appropriate data management software package; (databases)*

10a *evaluate how effective IT has been in meeting their needs in particular scientific contexts.*

Each of these is couched in fairly general terms with flexibility for choosing the actual lesson context. Worthy of particular note is the fact that the subjects also follow this non-specific approach while the illustrative examples are used to suggest activities, based on IT tools, which might be used in the classroom. For example although the statements of attainment appear to focus only on word processing in English, the examples given with the statements include mention of databases and desk top publishing while electronic mail is mentioned in the programmes of study.

The clear message is that we still have much freedom to choose the context of our lessons. The provisos are that the learning experiences satisfy the guidelines of the programmes of study and that the pupils' work is assessable according to the outcomes specified by the attainment targets.

TACKLING IT IN THE CURRICULUM

Finding appropriate and meaningful activities for inclusion of IT in our lessons requires some thought. According to the theory, history teachers who announce to class 4B that 'Today we are going to do databases ...' must be wrong - or must they be? There are many 4Bs who do not know how to use databases and it seems logical that they will require some training in their use before being let loose on them. Where these history teachers would be wrong is where they choose to teach databases per se instead of teaching history with the assistance of databases. The difference is not subtle.

With IT as a cross-curricular theme, the primary objective is not for it to be taught; rather it is to be assimilated naturally by finding appropriate uses in the learning experiences of the pupils. History's obligation to the development of a pupil's competence in IT is not to teach them about databases but is to provide them with opportunities to use, and appreciate the use of, databases in their learning of history. There are many examples of this latter approach. Once a historical context is chosen for class project work there will be a search for primary and secondary information sources that will very often throw up significant amounts of 'data'. Part of the historical analyst's task is to evaluate this data, to categorize and structure it to get the maximum amount of information from it.

Pupils can become very enthusiastic and industrious in their projects, particularly in local studies, and the amount of material that requires analysis can be awe inspiring. The first level of analysis - codifying or classifying the data - is a major learning activity that is in fact also an aspect of learning to use databases. In making a new database there has to be a data gathering activity followed by a classification of the data. Once prepared the classification will be divided into headings that will then be used to provide the structure of the database.

History, of course, has no exclusive hold on databases. Take an example that could feature in many maths classes - a survey of the types of cars available in the pupils' locality. Depending on the type of instructions given, and how well the pupils follow them, the type of information arising from such a pupil survey can be very varied. Some pupils will come back with the minimum of details, for example only the colour and manufacturer. Others will provide more comprehensive details such as body type (e.g. saloon, estate and so on), model type (e.g. XR3i, Popular Plus and so on) registration number, mileage (as read from the speedometer from the outside), engine type (e.g. diesel or petrol) and special features such as four wheel drive or turbo charging. They will inevitably have different classifications for the same information e.g. 'body type' may be called 'shape', or 'model' or 'design' and so on. But don't rule out the benefits in gathering the data first and learning the lesson that people can observe the same thing yet see it in different ways.

Whether the classification is carried out before or after the data collection, the classification process must be worked through in order to structure the information. A simple classification with some examples might be:

Car record no.	1	2	3	4
Manufacturer	Ford	Mazda	Ford	Vauxhall
Model	Escort	626	Anglia	Belmont
Body	Saloon	Hatchback	Saloon	Saloon
Engine type	Petrol	petrol	Petrol	Diesel
Engine size	1.6	2.0	Knot known	1.8
Registration	XYY 148	YBA432	AB222	XYZ2345
Colour	Red	Grey	Blue	Bronze
Mileage	20240	6064	15362	18653
Features	R. Spoiler	Executive	None	None

In a typical maths class this information could run to 300 cars or more (say 10 cars per pupil). If the teacher wants simply to examine the share of the local market that each manufacturer has then this would be a simple process of totalling the frequencies for each and expressing the results as a percentage. A pie-chart would be an effective means of illustrating the breakdown. If the data is need to be analysed more thoroughly e.g. if what is required is the proportion of saloons compared to hatchbacks, or the proportion of 1.3 litre engines or the number of cars with car telephones then the work quickly mounts up to a lot of repetitive paper shuffling. Given only one source of information (literally a pile of 300-plus pupil survey i.e. data collection sheets) for the whole class clearly searching them more than once can be a tedious task. With access limited to one or two nominees who have to search the data for each answer, every interrogation of the paper database becomes a long drawn out process. Clearly there is justification for using a computerised database in such a case. Once the information is typed in (a job that, it is only fair to say, can take a fair amount of time in itself) the database is quickly and easily interrogated.

Although each system will have its own variations, the interrogation process will be such that the computer obeys a command similar to the following, in terms of its structure and function:
FIND Manufacturer EQUAL TO Ford AND Engine size GREATER THAN 1.3.

The data will be searched almost instantly and in most cases options for listing the results on screen or printing them on paper will be offered. Once in magnetic form (i.e. stored on a computer disk) the data may be used by other classes. As such it may provide a focus for cross-subject collaboration but this will depend largely on the interest of the other teachers, the curricular relevance that can be found in it for other subject needs and the time and effort required to organize the collaboration.

Geography teachers might, for example, be interested in investigating the proportions of home and foreign built cars in the survey. In collaboration with science teachers, the geographers may also be interested in examining the amount of fossil fuels these cars use in a year.

In the mathematics class the analysis might extend to investigating the average mileage driven by car owners per year. As long as the registration number is known it is possible to estimate the age of the car, taking care to explain the possibility of re-registration and 'round-the-clock' mileages for cars like the Anglia cited. For example, registrations beginning with XY might have been released in the second half of 1988 while two-letter registrations beginning with A might have been released only in 1967.

Clearly an extra heading, e.g. Age, would be required in the database list once the year of registration is estimated for each car. The fuel and emission analyses would, however, normally require the data to be sorted into engine types and sizes.

CONCLUSION

There can be no dodging because the prescriptive approach to IT in the curriculum has major implications for the way teachers plan and carry out their teaching. How can pupils choose an IT tool 'naturally' to assist them in their learning if the teachers have never explored a machine and are even maybe a little bit fearful of or indeed openly hostile to IT. The curriculum and its cross curricular IT presents teachers therefore with a series of challenges. The success of the curriculum may be well related to the achievement of children in the cross-curricular themes.

ECONOMIC AWARENESS IN THE NORTHERN IRELAND CURRICULUM

Pat McNally

INTRODUCTION

Economic Awareness is a relatively new educational issue and its inclusion as a statutory theme in the Northern Ireland Curriculum follows six years of Department of Education sponsored development work. Mention of it frequently provokes a reaction of I could do with some of that. This in itself is a good sign; the rationale for assigning Economic Awareness such an important position in the curriculum requires less explanation. Frequently erroneous associations are made with the government of the day's political philosophy, but after a decade when ideas such as popular capitalism, deregulation and self enterprise have been actively promoted, such associations by newcomers may appear logical. For some teachers Economic Awareness can be a contentious issue, particularly if they come to it with preconceived notions of its origin and aim. The purpose of this chapter is to illuminate aspects of the background thinking which contributed to its development and to explore some of the issues associated with its implementation as a cross-curricular theme.

TOWARDS ECONOMIC AWARENESS FOR ALL PUPILS

'Economic Awareness' has emerged as the accepted terminology to describe a component of economic education in general education. In the early phase of development work it was more commonly known as economic literacy. Following the School Curriculum Development Committee's interest in this area in 1986, Economic Awareness emerged as the accepted description, taken to mean a continuum which progresses from economic understanding to economic competence and capability.

Over the past twenty years agreement has grown concerning the need for general education to include an economic dimension. One early exponent of this idea was Lawton (1975) who contended that the economy was an essential part of culture and therefore formal education had a role in passing on aspects of it to subsequent generations. Her Majesty's Inspectorate (HMI) strongly supported the idea of 'economic competence' as a prerequisite for all citizens. In *Curriculum 11-16* (better known as the *Red Book*), they acknowledged that some people did not think that schools were appropriate places for instructing young people in economic competence but they placed the issue firmly on the education agenda when they posed the question :

Where else can this task be undertaken methodically for all citizens? In an industrial democracy, can we leave this task to mere chance, probably depriving vast numbers of people of an understanding of the very processes and issues that affect their lives as citizens and workers ?

Subsequent government statements, up to and including *Better Schools* (cmnd 9469, 1988), and the proposals for education reform, reaffirmed the commitment to a dimension of economics education as an entitlement of every pupil.

While successive government statements expressed intent, development work was pioneered by interested organisations and groups. In 1975 the Economics Association launched a major curriculum development project in economics education for 14 to 16 year olds. Interest had grown in economics as an option subject for pupils in the post 16 age group and research by Holley and Skelton (1976) indicated a gap in provision for younger pupils. The Economic Education 14-16 Project ran for approximately ten years until 1987 and was organised into three phases ; research, development and dissemination.

Initial development work in Northern Ireland, funded by the Department of Education in 1983, was linked to the dissemination phase of this project and adopted its philosophy of economics education as part of the entitlement curriculum of every pupil. This locally based work was subsequently extended with the establishment of the Economics Education Project under the auspices of the Northern Ireland Council for Educational Development (NICED 1984-

1989) and the designation of Economic Awareness as a priority in the Vocational Education Programme (1987).

A DEFINITION OF ECONOMIC AWARENESS

The definition of Economic Awareness has been a much debated issue. Early government statements emphasised a functionalist approach, for example the 1977 Green Paper, Education in Schools stated that curricular provision needed *to help children appreciate how a nation earns and maintains its standard of living* while later statements such as the 1980 HMI *A View of Curriculum* referred to the need to enable pupils to enter the world after formal education is over as active participants in society and as responsible contributors to it, capable of achieving as much independence as possible. Several views co-existed; some stressed preparation for adult life in the world as it is (or was), while others were keen that pupils should develop a degree of personal autonomy which would equip them for the world they would know.

The *Red Book* made an early contribution to the debate by recommending that the curriculum should not be planned and constructed in terms of subject labels only that it was necessary to look beyond the subject discipline to the areas of experience and knowledge to which it may provide access and to the skills and attitudes that it may assist to develop. Inclusion of the social and political area of experience confirmed HMI support for the inclusion of an economic dimension in the education of all pupils.

The Economics Association was one of many subject associations to respond to HMI's request for information on the contribution to the areas of experience. Their response contained in a paper entitled, *The Contribution of Economics Education to General Education* (1977), presented a strong case for including elements of economics in general education, or in the common core of the curriculum.

The argument centred on three main points:

economic knowledge, concepts and skills are needed to enable all young people to better understand the world in which they live, and the sophisticated workings of their own economy;

the need to develop an understanding of the more important economic forces and institutions with which everyone comes into contact as producers and consumers, and of the critical interdependence of economic actions;

ensuring that sufficient knowledge of economics and the methods of social science are acquired to enable full participation in the decision making processes of a modern industrial democracy.

These points clearly outlined the parameters of the debate on the nature of Economic Awareness and provided a framework around which subsequent development work was planned.

The contribution of the Economics Education 14-16 Project was significant in helping teachers to provide stimulating and relevant classroom experiences on economic issues. The exemplar materials devised during phase two of the Project were designed for use within separate subject courses in economics and other unidisciplinary and multidisciplinary, social and commercial subjects. They focused on economic concepts and issues relating to the economic roles of young people as consumers, producers and citizens. The role orientated framework was devised in response to the findings of the initial research. This had indicated that the best approach for teaching economic ideas to younger pupils, particularly the low attainers, was through courses in personal economics. It was felt that pupils would relate directly to the notion of roles as being relevant to their lives and that it would help to emphasise the idea of interdependence in the economy. This role orientated description of the young person as consumer, producer and citizen has become an accepted part of the terminology of economics education.

Other dimensions built into the materials were the aims of developing appropriate skills and attitudes to economics education, and encouraging teachers to use active, learner-orientated, enquiry based approaches. Contact teachers in Northern Ireland, like their counterparts in other regions, reported positive progress in assimilating such approaches into normal teaching programmes and in terms of their professional development.

The direction of development work undertaken by the NICED Project was influenced by the progress of the Economics Education 14-16 Project that had reached its dissemination phase. From the outset work focused on the dual role of trying to extend the network of contact teachers and of raising awareness of the need to include a dimension of economics education in the curriculum of all pupils.

Early attention was given to the preparation of a statement that aimed to provide a definition of Economic Awareness and to outline a rationale for its inclusion in the entitlement curriculum of all pupils. The publication of *Economic Awareness: an Approach for Schools* (NICED 1985) was widely distributed within the development network and at that time made a significant contribution to the national debate on 'what is Economic Awareness ?' Implicit in the guidance contained in this document was the idea that economics education should aim to develop more than functionalist understanding and skills pertinent to the needs of individuals in an economy. It stressed the development of knowledge, understanding and skills required by young people to participate in a complex economic environment where everyone confronts decisions concerning the allocation of limited resources. Contexts for inquiry were suggested ranging from money management to analysis of the personal implications of government policies. The emphasis was on resource allocation in general, not just the area of personal finance.

The aim of a programme in Economic Awareness was stated as trying to equip young people with the insights into the ways in which economic events and decisions impinged on their lives and to recognise the personal and social implications of such phenomena in the future. Reference to 'the economic facts of life' further emphasised the basic importance of the area to everyday life. It stressed the need to empower young people to make decisions about the best use of resources and to be able to communicate their views to others. The ideas outlined in this paper clarified notions on the nature of economics education needed by pupils to make sense of their economic environment and to encourage participation in it.

Defining Economic Awareness has not been easy. Early explanations tended to stress pupil achievement and outcomes, and indicate appropriate learning experiences. A statement from the Economic Awareness Teacher Training Programme (EcATT) illustrates this point. The rationale is that everyone is involved in the economic system:

We all face the problem of deciding how best to allocate our limited resources. An economically aware person needs the skills, information and concepts to assess the implications of individual and group decisions.

Evidence drawn from work with pupils indicated that meaningful learning experiences were those in which they were introduced to an issue or context using an appropriate stimulus or experience, and encouraged to engage in a process of reflection.

Prior to the introduction of education reform, schools chose the mode of delivery for Economic Awareness and, indeed, decided whether or not to include it in their curricular provision at all. In Northern Ireland a range of implementation strategies were tried. Initially modular courses were popular (see Hodkinson and Dunnill 1988 Chapters 7,12 and 13) and later implementation in subjects. The introduction of the General Certificate in Secondary Education(GCSE) and in particular the requirement of National Criteria that all subjects should *be relevant to the candidate's own life and develop an awareness of economic... factors* had increased the opportunities to develop Economic Awareness. The government's decision to base the common curriculum in Northern Ireland on six Areas of Study, with cross-curricular themes woven into the attainment targets and programmes of study of the designated subject(s) for each area, finalised the debate on the mode of delivery and helped to concentrate thinking on the relationships between Economic Awareness and particular subjects.

ECONOMIC AWARENESS IN THE CURRICULUM

The inclusion of Economic Awareness in the new curricular framework is a welcome development and further indicates government commitment to this area. Given the dialogue concerning the definition of Economic Awareness, the remit given to the Ministerial Working Group in 1989 presented a great challenge. They were asked essentially to define the 'content of Economic Awareness' and to make recommendations as to its delivery within the compulsory and other subjects in the curriculum. Building on the ideas outlined earlier, agreement was reached at an early stage as to the general aim of Economic Awareness in the curriculum. This was outlined as follows:

Economic Awareness as an educational theme aims to develop in young people the ability to participate effectively in the economy as confident consumers, producers and citizens.

This led to some pertinent questions being posed. What abilities do young people need to participate effectively in the economy as confident consumers, producers and citizens ? How can these abilities be developed through the prescribed and other subjects in the curriculum ?

The conclusion was that the 'recommended content' should be expressed in terms of an Economic Awareness capability, defined as two learning outcomes, and four areas of Experience and Understanding, as outlined in the table below. The learning outcomes were subsequently termed objectives by the Northern Ireland Curriculum Council (NICC). Together these describe the abilities needed by young people to participate effectively in the economy. The four areas of experience and understanding mapped out the contexts in which this capability should be applied. It was considered necessary for young people to have experience of all four areas to ensure the breadth of experience needed to relate to the range of issues that impinge on everyday life.

ECONOMIC AWARENESS CAPABILITY
Learning Outcomes

Young people should be able to use appropriate knowledge, understanding and skills to evaluate economic information and ideas, including their presentation in words, images, graphs and statistics.

AND

Young people should be able to use appropriate knowledge, understanding and skills to be able to make balanced and informed judgements and, where necessary, know the appropriate action to take on issues, problems and events where there is an economic dimension.

AREAS OF EXPERIENCE AND UNDERSTANDING

The Individual in the Economy
The Business Community
The Local, National & European Communities
The International Community

The Recommended Content for Economic Awareness in the Northern
Ireland Curriculum

Reference to developing the understanding, skills and knowledge
needed to evaluate economic information, which could be presented
in a variety of forms, stemmed from the view that everyone needs to
be able to assess both the personal and the wider of decisions that
have resource implications. Nowadays economic information is
presented in a variety of forms and transmitted through different
media, both of which can influence the understanding of the
message or idea. Reference to the presentation of ideas and
information in words, images, graphs and statistics, acknowledged
the influence of the form of presentation. Perhaps the best illustration
of this relates to the impact of advertising. Increasingly young people
need to be able to discern the subtle messages transmitted through
advertisements, to question the values that underpin persuasive
forms of advertising and to assess the relevance of such messages for
the constrained choices that they have to make in everyday life. The
need to make balanced and informed judgements reflects the aim of
encouraging pupils to become active participants in the economy,
capable of making informed decisions on issues, problems or events
where there is an economic dimension.

A list of characteristics of attainment associated with the learning
outcomes was provided to clarify further the process needed to tease
out the economic dimension of an issue, problem or event. Teachers
have responded positively to this guidance as it has provided prompt
statements around which issues can be explored. These
characteristics indicate that pupils should be able to:

*locate, identify and describe economic information and the ways in
which it is presented;*

*analyse and interpret economic information and the ways in which
it is presented;*

*assess the reliability and limitations of economic information by
comparing it with other available and relevant information;*

identify the competing priorities relating to the use of available resources which arise from different values and alternative viewpoints;

recognise that practical solutions to the problem of deciding between competing priorities may require compromises to be made;

analyse and compare the economic costs and benefits when deciding whether one course of action, or judgement, is better than another;

assess the reliability and limitations of evidence used in deciding between alternative courses of action or judgements.

The reference to 'economic information' in the learning outcomes has required clarification as some interpretations have been based on the perception that the term 'economic' must relate to economic theory or high finance. The intention was that this term would refer to all the information used in the decision making process where there is an economic dimension. In science students may be asked to assess the costs and benefits of different methods of conserving energy in the home. The information needed to explore this issue will include the types of energy used in the home, the energy consumption of appliances and facilities, and the various actions which can be taken to minimise its use and maximise its benefits. In this situation, the essential scientific information on energy consumption and conservation is also relevant information which young people must evaluate and use to make a balanced and informed economic judgement on the costs and benefits of the vaarious options. In other subject areas information that is immediately categorised as generic to specific subjects, such as geographic or historical information, will also be used alongside essentially economic information to analyse and evaluate the economic dimension.

The economic dimension is just one perspective that is brought to bear in making choices but it may not always be the factor that determines the final decision. Other factors need to be considered, such as health and environmental implications, and the final choice will reflect an individual's value system. Promoting Economic Awareness encourages people to include an economic dimension in their everyday decision making and to be aware of the values that underpin their choices.

Direct use of economic terminology was avoided in outlining the 'recommended content' although many economic concepts are implied in the learning outcomes and the characteristics of attainment (scarcity and choice, opportunity cost, cost-benefit analysis). It was felt that teachers needed to see the theme as a natural aspect of their subjects and something that would enhance the subject, rather than as a bolted on section from an economics syllabus. This approach differed from that taken by the National Curriculum Council in Curriculum Guidance Four, (1990). This presented a 'harder' economic outline of their equivalent theme that led one observer to comment that it offered a pretty convincing impersonation of a subject. (*Mackenzie Education*, 2 November, 1990)

ECONOMIC AWARENESS AND SUBJECT LINKS

In the course of work, analysis conducted by the cross-curricular Working Group of existing practice in subjects indicated that the description of Economic Awareness capability was relevant in the full range of subject areas and consistent with good practice. Further analysis relating to the areas of experience and understanding concluded that economic issues were already an aspect of many subjects, possibly assisted by the requirements of GCSE criteria. The Group concluded that subject specialists should determine the contexts within which Economic Awareness could be developed. The final recommendation given to Subject Working Groups was that their attainment targets should reflect the essence of Economic Awareness capability and that their programmes of study should consider relevant issues from the four broad area of experience and understanding. While acknowledging that Subject Working Groups would be better placed to determine the contexts in which Economic Awareness could be developed, examples of possible subject learning outcomes were suggested. These were presented as in the examples below.

Young people should have opportunities

to analyse and interpret information used in advertising and the ways in which it is presented, and to assess the reliability and limitations of this information when deciding between alternative courses of action or judgements (English);

to assess the consequences on personal and family finance of changes in income and/or prices, including the implications of the true cost of borrowing, when making consumer choices(mathematics);

to assess the effects on the food chain and the costs and benefits to the consumer of intensive methods of production in agriculture (science).

So far the reports of the Subject Working Groups indicate a positive response to incorporating Economic Awareness. The mathematics Report stated clearly that Economic Awareness (and information Technology) impinged more than the other themes on the mathematics curriculum. One of the fundamental goals of mathematics is stated as helping pupils to appreciate the usefulness of mathematics in everyday life. There is much common ground between the description of the contribution of science to the whole curriculum (Section 2.3 of the Proposals for the Science Curriculum) and the 'recommended content' for Economic Awareness. The processes associated with attainment target one, exploring and investigating science, are consistent with developing Economic Awareness capability and economic issues pervade most attainment targets, without the inclusion of additional content. The programmes of study for English specify economic contexts including the need for pupils to have opportunities to:

use role play and simulations and explore social and economic issues (Talking and Listening, key stage 3) and
encounter a wide variety of texts including some directed at their own age group and some directed at adults, for example consumer reports, newspapers... (Reading, key stage 4)

The description of the Programme of Study for English gives more flexibility to teachers to determine the contexts to select as a focus for their work in reading, writing, talking and listening. The emphasis on developing Economic Awareness capability centres on the idea that if pupils have gained experience and confidence in approaching economic issues in this way, they will be better able to transfer this ability to new and less familiar contexts that they are likely to encounter as they progress through life. It is consistent development of Economic Awareness capability that will form the basis of a coherent programme for pupils as they progress through each key stage.

KEY STAGE PROGRESSION

Economic Awareness has been designated as a mandatory theme at key stages 3/4 only, and a strong recommendation from the Cross Curricular Working Group that it should be extended to key stages 1/2 was not endorsed by either NICC or by the Minister for Education. The advice, however, is that it should be developed where appropriate in the primary curriculum, which incidentally was the basis of all the initial recommendations. The resulting situation has presented an anomaly in provision between Northern Ireland and other regions, where Economic and Industrial Understanding is being developed in the National Curriculum in England and Wales from ages five to sixteen. Several Subject Working Groups have reported that Economic Awareness is included in the recommended curriculum for key stages 1/2, notably mathematics, science and geography, yet many primary practitioners perceive it as being of little to relevance to their work. The official funding and support of enterprise education and industrial projects in the primary sector appears to contradict views on the value and relevance of Economic Awareness for this age group.

Since processes consistent with developing Economic Awareness capability and the issues outlined in four areas of experience and understanding are equally relevant to younger pupils, issues will be revisited throughout experience in school. The Working Group concluded that the following factors would be important in distinguishing between attainment at ages 14 and 16:

the complexity of the task;
the number of issues and variables to be considered;
the quality and nature of the information used;
the degree of teacher intervention needed to complete a task.

It was suggested that teachers could help the learning process by careful planning tasks and by intelligent selection of the type and quantity of information to be used.

IMPLEMENTING ECONOMIC AWARENESS IN THE NORTHERN IRELAND CURRICULUM: Issues for Classroom Teachers and Curriculum Managers

As more essential curriculum documentation becomes available as subject reports and guidance material, evidence of opportunities to include Economic Awareness in the curriculum increases. What are individual subject teachers being asked to do ? What structures and procedures are being put in place to support teachers in their work and to monitor pupil progress? How is the general picture taking shape ?

Programmes of study and attainment targets present teachers with a framework around which they are required to provide appropriate learning experiences. Reactions to including Economic Awareness can vary considerably between subject groups and individual teachers, depending on factors such as experience of relevant development work or the constraining pressures of completing a syllabus. Teachers from some subject areas, notably geography, react positively since they already deal with economic issues in their work. Affirmative responses from teachers of other subjects are increasing, particularly if they have had the time and support needed to review work and plan ahead.

Specific references to Economic Awareness are evident in the new documentation. One example from the key stage 4 mathematics curriculum is the requirement that pupils should evaluate a simple business plan. Planning work in response to such references is just part of the mapping process. In addition teachers can select economic contexts in which to set work, hence increasing the relevance of their subjects to everyday life. One further illustration from mathematics concerns problems which focus on planning transport routes. These are a common setting for investigations on nodes and networks, yet transport networks are not mentioned in the programmes of study or the attainment targets. Cognisance of the relevant business objectives and procedures is a necessary part of the making this work meaningful and relevant to everyday life.

Analysis of curriculum documents indicates that both approaches are needed. When planning work teachers first need to:

identify economic contexts which arise within the subject and follow these through; and/or
identify opportunities where economic contexts can be included and follow these through.

Once a context for work has been identified, they need to ensure that the teaching/learning experiences are consistent with developing Economic Awareness capability.

Many schools have appointed a co-ordinator for Economic Awareness as an initial response to supporting development work. The range of activities undertaken by co-ordinators can vary considerably, from responsibility for disseminating information at one limited extreme, to working closely with colleagues in support of their development work at the other. Curriculum change has brought with it a need to appraise some roles and relationships. What is the role of a co-ordinator when heads of departments are charged with ensuring that their subjecs are making an adequate contribution ? In some schools the co-ordinator has been asked to catalogue work with successive year groups as a way of assembling the official record of Economic Awareness across subjects. In addition to this reactive role, there is still a need to be pro-active - knowing that Economic Awareness is a requirement and having access to statutory orders may not ensure that it becomes a reality for pupils. Some co-ordinators express frustration that their duties have not been specifically defined by management but, in practice, it is a role which is likely to evolve over time.

Management has a key role to play. The extent to which Economic Awareness is developed in the curriculum will depend on the opportunities provided for teachers to gain confidence and experience in handling this theme in their normal classroom work. Curriculum development work needs to be fostered in a climate of mutual support and understanding. School managers can facilitate this by creating the circumstances in which teachers can plan, review and share experiences of work. They can establish procedures for planning, organising and reviewing progress as well as paying attention to human factors by allaying fears and instilling confidence. Finally, progress will be reflected in pupil work and against established goals and procedures.

MATHEMATICS 1980-90: THE COCKCROFT DECADE

Clifford Boyd and Martin Fitzpatrick

INTRODUCTION

In January 1982 the Report of the Committee of Inquiry into the Teaching of Mathematics in Schools was published. It was entitled *Mathematics Counts* but it is more commonly called the *Cockcroft Report* after its chairman, Dr. W. H. Cockcroft. The committee had been set up in 1978 with the following terms of reference:

To consider the teaching of mathematics in primary and secondary schools in England and Wales, with particular reference to the mathematics required in further and higher education, employment and adult life generally, and to make recommendations. (Cockcroft 1982)

It may seem strange to begin a discussion of school mathematics in Northern Ireland during the last decade by referring to a report relating to England and Wales. It is our contention, however, that the *Cockcroft Report* has had a profound influence on developments in school mathematics in this province in that period, culminating in the Northern Ireland Curriculum mathematics legislation in 1990. The developments we have in mind, other than the 1990 legislation, are the introduction into primary schools of the NICED Mathematics Guidelines for Primary Schools in 1984 and the establishment in the secondary sector of the NISEC GCSE Mathematics scheme in 1986.

In 1980 the DENI Inspectorate carried out a survey of primary education in the province. Following the observations contained in the survey report, NICED was asked to produce a set of guidelines for the different curricular areas in primary schools. Those responsible for the guidelines in mathematics were able to carry out their deliberations in the full knowledge of the conclusions and recommendations of the *Cockcroft Report*. That the report had considerable influence on the content of the guidelines is borne out by the many references to it in the guidelines document itself.

In 1985, following the government's decision that the GCE and CSE examinations at 16+ be merged into a new single GCSE examination, the DES and the Welsh Office issued a statement of National Criteria for Mathematics, setting out the essential requirements that had to be satisfied by all syllabuses for GCSE examinations entitled Mathematics. It was the responsibility of the different examining groups, including NISEC, to determine their syllabuses and techniques of assessment in accordance with these criteria. That the Cockcroft Report would have a significant influence on all GCSE Mathematics schemes was guaranteed by the requirement in the National Criteria that:

When devising examinations in Mathematics regard should be paid to the discussion and recommendations to be found in the Report of the Committee of Inquiry into the Teaching of Mathematics in Schools (The Cockcroft Report).

In 1990 the Northern Ireland Curriculum Mathematics scheme became part of the law of the land. That scheme derived essentially from the report of the Mathematics Working Group commissioned by DENI in 1989 to bring in proposals for programmes of study and attainment targets. In the group's report (NICC 1989) clearly there was a desire to build on and not replace the best practices arising out of the NICED Mathematics Guidelines for Primary Schools and the NISEC GCSE scheme.

In what follows we show in detail how the Cockcroft Report has influenced, in turn, the developments in 1984, 1986 and 1990. We start by considering what the report had to say about the following fundamental questions:

Why teach mathematics?
What mathematics should be taught?
How should mathematics be taught?
How should mathematics learning be assessed?

We then consider how Cockcroft ideas permeated what the NICED Mathematics Guidelines for Primary Schools, the NISEC GCSE scheme and the Northern Ireland Curriculum Mathematics legislation had to say in answer to the same questions. The order in which the questions are addressed in considering each of the three developments will vary as appropriate.

THE COCKCROFT REPORT (COCKCROFT 1982)

Why teach mathematics?

The report summarised its position on the reasons for teaching mathematics in schools by offering the following description of the teacher's task:

In our view the mathematics teacher has the task
. *of enabling each pupil to develop, within his capabilities, the mathematical skills and understanding required for adult life, for employment and for further study and training ...*
. *of providing each pupil with such mathematics as may be needed for his study of other subjects;*
. *of helping each pupil to develop as far as possible his appreciation and enjoyment of mathematics itself and his realisation of the role hat it has played and will continue to play both in the development of science and technology and of our civilisation;*
. *above all, of making each pupil aware that mathematics provides him with a powerful means of communication.* (para 12)

The order above is significant, clearly indicating the utilitarian perspective on school mathematics that the report largely adopted; in this regard it is also significant that the order of priority in the terms of reference (quoted above) is reversed in citing in the first reason the mathematical needs of adult life, employment and further study and training.

What mathematics should be taught?

The report welcomed the widening of the curriculum that had taken place in most primary schools during the previous twenty years to include *a greater understanding of number and also work on measurement, shape and space, graphical representation and the development of simple logical ideas* (para 286).

It acknowledged, however, the existence of pressure in some quarters for a 'back to basics' movement:

This has encouraged some primary teachers and some teachers of low-attaining pupils in secondary schools to restrict their teaching largely to the attainment of computational skills. (para 278)

In Northern Ireland the DENI primary survey (DENI 1981)also recognised that there had been a widening of approach but still found that *in more than one-fifth of classes, excessive time is being spent on repetitive calculation (paragraph 3.28).* The Cockcroft committee rejected the notion of a narrow concentration on computational skill, pushing instead for a broad spectrum of mathematics to be taught to all pupils, both primary and secondary:

... the ability to carry out a particular numerical operation and the ability to know when to use it are not the same; both are needed. The mathematics of employment and of everyday life is always mathematics in context...Arithmetical skills are therefore a tool for use in situations that require an understanding of other areas of mathematics, for example the geometry of shape and space and graphical representation of various kinds. An excessive concentration on the purely mechanical skills of arithmetic for their sake will not assist the development of understanding in these other areas.
...emphasis on arithmetical skills does not of itself lead to the ability to make use of these skills in practical situations. It is only within a broadly based curriculum that the ability to apply mathematics is enabled to develop. (paragraphs 278 and 288)

The report promoted as fundamental the principle that in school mathematics *no topic should be included unless it can be developed sufficiently for it to be applied in ways that pupils can understand (paragraph 451)* and argued for the need relate the content of the mathematics course to pupil's experience of everyday life (para 462). These ideas are fleshed out in the report's 'foundation list' of mathematical topics to be included in the mathematics syllabus for

Number, Money, Percentages, Use of a Calculator, Time, Measurement, Graphs and Pictorial Representation, Spatial Concepts, Ratio and Proportion, Statistical Ideas.

Although it rejected a narrow concentration on computational skills the report did strongly advocate flexibility in approaches to calculation. Noting that there had been a decline of mental and oral work within mathematics classrooms, the Cockcroft committee argued for a greater prominence to be given to 'mental calculation':

We believe that the decline of mental and oral work within mathematics classrooms represents a failure to recognise the central place which working 'done in the head' occupies throughout mathematics. Even when using traditional methods of recording calculations on paper, the written record is usually based on steps that are done mentally... However, a more important reason for including the practice of mental calculation is the now well established fact that those who are mathematically effective in daily life seldom make use 'in their heads' of the standard written methods that are used in the classroom, but either adapt them in a personal way or make use of methods that are highly idiosyncratic. (paragraphs 255 and 256)

(A similar decline in mental work had been observed in the DENI primary survey, in which it was noted that *Such work appears to have been given less attention since the broadening of the mathematical curriculum* (DENI 1981, para 3.29).)

The Cockcroft Report also gave encouragement to the use of methods of written calculations other than the traditional ones:

Although there are occasions on which it can be both quick and convenient to carry out written calculations in the traditional way, 'back of an envelope' methods are often not only quicker but more straightfoward....
Discussion of such alternative methods with a group or class provides valuable opportunity for developing confidence and 'feel' when doing number work. (para 263 and 265)

As for calculators the report commended their use in both primary and secondary schools:

...it is right that primary teachers should allow children to make use of calculators for appropriate purposes...
...there is one over-riding reason why all secondary pupils should, as part of their mathematics course, be taught and allowed to use a calculator. This arises from the increasing use that is being made of calculators both in employment and in adult life.
(para 387 and 389)

Overall a balance was advocated between calculations carried out mentally, on paper, or with a calculator. As the 'foundation list' in paragraph 458 put it:

Pupils should possess some reliable method (however unconventional) of carrying out calculations without the use of a calculator when the numbers are small, and with a calculator when larger numbers are involved. There is a need to develop and encourage intuitive methods of both written and mental calculation

How should mathematics be taught?

The most often quoted section of the Cockcroft Report is paragraph 243 that deals with classroom practice, suggesting that mathematics teaching at all levels should include opportunities for:

exposition by the teacher
discussion between teacher and pupils and between pupils themselves
appropriate practical work
consolidation and practice of fundamental skills and routines
problem solving, including the application of mathematics to everyday situations
investigational work.

The committee was aware that it was not saying anything new:

The list we have given has appeared, by implication if not explicitly, in official reports, DES publications, HMI discussion documents and the journals and publications of the professional mathematical associations, Yet we are aware that although there are some classrooms in which the teaching includes, as a matter of course, all the elements we have listed, there are still many in which the mathematics teaching does not include even a majority of these elements.

What was meant by this last statement was that in many classrooms the traditional styles of exposition and occasional controlled discussion, usually teacher-led if not teacher-dominated, were the norm, the bulk of class time being used for consolidation and practice. Problem solving, practical work and investigational work were much more rare. There is no evidence to suggest that the situation was any different in classrooms in Northern Ireland. The DENI primary survey noted:

In the majority of P5 and P7 classes, the teaching approach is didactic, with emphasis on clear, careful exposition by the teacher at the chalkboard followed by written exercises from textbooks...
In fewer classes than is desirable, is there evidence of children having carried out, over a period, sustained work on an investigation that has some mathematical content, or of having been encouraged to tackle some individual or group work on mathematical topics. (DENI 1981, para 3.23 and 3.41)

Yet paragraph 323 of the *Cockcroft Report* insisted that the development of general strategies directed towards problem solving and investigations could start during the primary years and set out the processes to be used in work of this kind:

One of these is to make a graphical or diagrammatic representation of the situation that is being investigated; for example, if two dice are being thrown, the scores obtained can be recorded graphically. There may be a pattern in the results that are being obtained that can lead to the making of a conjecture to forecast later results; for example, 2 points on a circle can be joined by one line, 3 points can be joined in pairs by 3 lines, 4 points by 6 lines and so on. Efforts can then be made to discover whether, and explain why, the conjecture is or is not correct. It is sometimes appropriate to set up an experiment, for example to discover the length of a seconds pendulum, or to employ the strategy of looking at a simpler related problem; an example of this latter strategy is that the number of squares (of any size) on a full-sized chessboard may be too many to count, but a 2 x 2 and a 3 x 3 board are more manageable, and a pattern begins to emerge. It is necessary to develop persistence in exploring a problem, for example the number of different shapes that can be made from a given number of squares of the same size, and the ability to record the possibilities that have been tried. Finally, it is important to develop the ability to work with others in the discussion of possible approaches and to be able to communicate progress that has been made by means of words, diagrams and symbols.

How should mathematics learning be assessed?

The Cockcroft Report recognised that reform of the examination system at 16+ was essential for the implementation of many of its recommendations for secondary schools:

the syllabuses which will be prescribed and the papers that will be set will be the greatest single factor in influencing the mathematics teaching in the coming years. (para 521)

It advocated two fundamental principles which should govern any assessment in mathematics.

The first is that the examination papers and other methods of assesssment that are used should be such that they enable candidates to demonstrate what they do know rather than what they do not know. The second is that the examinations should not undermine the confidence of those who attempt them. (paragraph 521)

The implication was that it would be essential to provide a number of different papers so that pupils could attempt those papers that were appropriate to their levels of attainment. The report also observed that :

Examinations in mathematics that consist only of timed written papers cannot ... assess ability to undertake practical and investigational work or ability to carry out work of an extended nature.

They cannot assess skills of mental computation or ability to discuss mathematics...Work ... of this kind can only be assessed in the classroom and such assessment needs to be made over an extended period.

...Not only do written examinations fail to assess work of the kind we have described... but, in cases where they comprise the only method of assessment, they lead teachers to emphasise in the classroom work of a kind which is directly related to the type of question that is set in the examination. This means that, especially as the examination approaches but often also from a much earlier stage, practical and investigational work finds no place in day-to-day work in mathematics.

...if assessment at 16+ is to reflect as many aspects of mathematical attainment as possible, it needs to take account not only of those aspects that it is possible to examine by means of written papers but also of those aspects which need to be assessed in another way. (para 532, 533 and 534)

Arguing that assessment procedures in public examinations should be such as to encourage good classroom practice the report recommended that provision should be made for an element of teacher assessment to be included in the examination of pupils of all levels of attainment (para 535).

THE NICED MATHEMATICS GUIDELINES FOR PRIMARY SCHOOLS (NICED 1984)

Why teach mathematics?

Four reasons were given for teaching mathematics, all of which may essentially be found in Cockcroft's paragraph 12 (quoted above):

Consideration might be given to the following reasons for teaching mathematics:
because of its use in everyday life
because it can be enjoyable
because of its value as a subject in its own right
because of its application to other subjects (p.1)

What mathematics should be taught?

Acknowledgement was made of 'the gap that exists between the importance attached to formal computation in school and the way we use numbers in everyday life'(p.13) and support for a broadly based curriculum was expressed in the recommendation that schools' schemes of work should contain 'a clear statement of progression through each area of the curriculum' (p.12), the areas of the curriculum being defined as:Number; Measurement; Shape; Pictorial and Graphic Representation. The Cockcroft ideas on flexibility in the approach to calculation were also reinforced:

A school is expected to teach a child standard methods of computation. However the ability to use personal methods and shortcuts in carrying out written and mental calculations could have more relevance in the age of calculators and computers. (p 14)

The Guidelines (p.53) went on to explicit publicity to the positive attitude towards calculators taken by the Cockcroft committee.

How should mathematics be taught?

The activities recommended in Cockcroft's paragraph 243 were publicised and endorsed (p43). In respect of problem solving, for example, explicit reference was made to the general strategies set out in paragraph 323 of the Cockcroft Report. Also included was a suggestion for a staff workshop on these strategies containing examples to be worked on by both teachers and pupils. (see Appendix 1)

How should mathematics learning be assessed?

Although primary pupils did not have to face any public examination in mathematics as such, the Guidelines did make some comments about assessment. In one such comment a concern of the Cockcroft Report was reiterated:

In many schools it consists of written tests and from such a narrow base can have a restrictive influence on the content of the curriculum. (p66)

THE NISEC GCSE MATHEMATICS SCHEME (NISEC 1986)

Why teach mathematics?

The scheme published in 1986 (for first examination in 1988) contained no explicit reference to any reasons for teaching mathematics in school. It did, however, set out a list of aims for any course in mathematics leading to the GCSE examination. That list included statements that such courses should enable pupils to:

2.4 apply mathematics in everyday situations and develop an understanding of the part which mathematics plays in the world around them...
2.8 use mathematics as a means of communication with emphasis on clear expression
2.9 develop an ability to apply mathematics in other subjects, particularly science and technology
2.12 produce and appreciate imaginative and creative work arising from mathematical ideas

It is not difficult to see herein substantial traces of Cockcroft's paragraph 12.

How should mathematics learning be assessed?

The National Criteria for Mathematics (DES and Welsh Office 1985) required all examination boards to reconstruct their mathematics examination systems to introduce a differentiated scheme whereby pupils of differing abilities and expectations could choose from various combinations of papers for which different grades might be awarded. The NISEC GCSE Mathematics scheme adopted a model of six written examination papers from which candidates would select a pair (Papers 1 & 2 for Basic level candidates who might achieve E, F or G grades, Papers 3 & 4 for Intermediate level candidates who might achieve C, D, E or F grades and Papers 5 & 6 for High level candidates who might achieve A, B, C or D grades). This model aims to ensure that few candidates encounter a paper designed for an ability group other than their own, thus providing almost all candidates with a reasonably satisfying examination experience. There is built into the papers, of course, an overlap that allows comparison between candidates being awarded a grade that is available from two different entry levels. The papers are designed with the intention that appropriately entered candidates should obtain between fifty and one hundred percent of the marks available.

The National Criteria for Mathematics, again in line with the Cockcroft Report, required the examination boards to broaden assessment to deal with aspects of mathematical performance not catered for by timed written examinations. As a result the NISEC GCSE Mathematics scheme contained the following assessment objectives, which required that pupils be tested in their ability to:

3.16 respond orally to questions about mathematics, discuss mathematical ideas and carry out mathematical exercises, including calculations, mentally;

3.17 carry out practical and investigational work, and undertake extended pieces of work..

The assessment of pupils' ability to carry out mathematical exercises, including calculations, mentally was achieved by the introduction of an aural and computation test (papers 7, 8, 9 at the three levels, again with overlap). An example of such a test is given in Appendix 2. The assessment of objective 3.17 and the oral and discussion aspects of 3.16 was to be accomplished through a teacher-assessed course work element. For candidates preparing for the examinations in 1988, 1989 and 1990 this was on an optional basis; pupils were able to enter for an examination 'with course work' or an examination 'without course work'.

What mathematics should be taught?

The introduction of the new GCSE syllabus considerably reinforced the idea of a broadly based curriculum for all pupils. The National Criteria for Mathematics set out a list of 'core' items, the so-called 'List 1' and 'List 2', which had to be incorporated, according to certain rules, into syllabuses bearing the title Mathematics. List 1 had to form almost the whole of the syllabus content for any examination that might lead to a candidate being awarded grade E (at maximum): Lists 1 and 2 had to form almost the whole of the syllabus content for any examination that might lead to a candidate being awarded grade C (at maximum). Not surprisingly List 1 bore a striking resemblance to Cockcroft's 'foundation list'. List 2 contained some natural extensions of the items in List 1.

The NISEC syllabus for Basic level pupils essentially consisted of topics in List 1; that for Intermediate level pupils contained little more than the sum of Lists 1 and 2; and that for High level candidates was an extension of the Intermediate syllabus. Cockcroft's flexible approach to calculation was promoted by expecting pupils to use calculators in their two written papers and by using the aural and computation test to assess mental and written calculations (carried out without calculators).

How should mathematics be taught?

Nothing was said explicitly about classroom practice. However the incorporation of assessment objectives 3.16 and 3.17 into the teacher-assessed course work element did lead to the inclusion of corresponding classroom work in fourth and fifth forms; naturally this worked its way down through the system as appropriate training, if nothing else, for pupils in lower secondary forms.

The delay in implementing compulsory GCSE course work applied only to mathematics and was a clear recognition of the scale of change being asked of teachers and pupils. It seemed to offer a golden opportunity for thorough in-service training in preparation for compulsory course work in 1991. Financial considerations unfortunately curtailed the possibilities. Nonetheless it was possible in 1986 for teachers to begin to prepare first form pupils for the fullblooded onslaught of GCSE mathematics which they would face in the 1991 examination.

NORTHERN IRELAND CURRICULUM MATHEMATICS (DENI 1990)

Why teach mathematics?

The statutory Northern Ireland Curriculum Mathematics document consists of two parts, namely the programmes of study and the attainment targets. No reference is made to any reasons for teaching mathematics. Such a discussion may, however, be found in the report of the Mathematics Working Group (NICC 1989). What that group did in its report was to reassert and amplify the four reasons set out in the NICED Mathematics Guidelines for Primary Schools.

What mathematics should be taught?

The programme of study for each of the four key stages set out the content and activities that pupils should encounter in order to learn mathematics, bearing in mind that different children reach different levels of achievement at different ages and that the mathematics they meet should be appropriate both to their age and to their progress to date. The idea of a broadly based curriculum for all pupils now became enshrined in legislation, as evidenced by the breadth of content (Number, Algebra, Measure, Shape and Space, Handling of Data) to be covered in the programmes of study. The same was true of the notion of flexibility in approaches to calculation. In the programme of study for Key Stage 2, for example, it is stated that:

In developing skills in pencil and paper calculations, children should devise personal ways of recording calculations, compare and discuss these, and ultimately refine and practise pencil and paper methods that are agreed and understood. At all times, however, a child's individual method of setting down work will have value; such personal methods should be encouraged and discussed.
The children's ability to adopt mental methods of calculation should be systematically developed as they acquire the basic arithmetical skills.....
Children should use calculators sensibly at a level appropriate to their ability.

How should mathematics learning be assessed?

The attainment targets (each containing a list of statements of attainment spanning up to ten levels) set standards against which pupils' achievement in their programmes of study are to be measured. At the time of writing the precise way of measuring that achievement at different levels across the attainment targets has not been finalised by NISEAC. What seems clear, however, is that the assessment at each of the key stages will contain a substantial teacher-assessed component. In particular in key stage 4 the main instrument of assessment will be a revised form of the GCSE examination that pupils will continue to enter at one of three levels (at least).

How should mathematics be taught?

When the statutory programmes of study were published in 1990 it became a legal requirement that each pupil should be involved in a wide range of purposeful activities, including essentially all of those pupil activities described in paragraph 243 of the Cockcroft Report. For example the key stage 4 statement of 'General Approach' could not embrace more fully the Cockcroft philosophy:

Pupils should regularly experience success in mathematics to help them to develop confidence and a positive attitude towards the subject.

Pupils should engage in activities that are balanced between different modes of learning. They should be doing, observing, discussing with other pupils and the teacher, reflecting, drafting, reading and recording.

Pupils should learn through tasks that develop knowledge, skills and understanding and also through tasks that develop their ability to tackle practical problems, working individually and in groups, presenting mathematics to which each pupil can claim ownership. They should engage in activities that allow them to develop their personal qualities. These should be balanced between those that are short in duration and those that have scope for development over an extended period. They should be both of the kind which have an exact answer or result and those that have many possible outcomes. Pupils should be involved in:

- *selecting materials and mathematics appropriate for a particular task;*

- *planning and working methodically;*

- *reviewing progress at appropriate stages;*

- *checking that results are sensible;*

- *using trial and improvement methods;*

- *trying alternative strategies;*

- *making and testing predictions;*

- *generalising;*

- *conjecturing, defining, proving and disproving.*

Pupils should develop their ability to communicate their mathematics by:

- *making sense of a task;*

- *interpreting mathematical information;*

- *talking about work-in-progress and asking questions;*

- *presenting results in an intelligible way to others.*

Moreover, an attainment target which was not content-based, namely P1 (Processes in Mathematics), was included. This meant that all pupils would be assessed on their ability to use mathematical processes in practical tasks, real-life problems and investigations within mathematics itself. The NICC Mathematics Guidance Materials made it clear that classroom activities compared with P1 should not be treated in isolation from the other attainment targets. (NICC 1990, p.26). It was now the obvious intention that the assessment procedure should complement, indeed possibly augment, the teaching and should encourage rather than hinder the use of the fullest range of approaches and classroom activities. What had been partially achieved at GCSE for pupils in key stage 4 was to be built upon and carried to the other key stages.

CONCLUSION

In summary, the last decade has seen schools in Northern Ireland update their mathematics curricula both as a natural ongoing activity and as a response to the NICED Mathematics Guidelines for Primary schools (in the primary sector), the NISEC GCSE scheme (in the secondary sector) and the Northern Ireland Curriculum Mathematics legislation (in both sectors). In this chapter we have shown how the Cockcroft Report has had a profound influence on these three developments.

The task facing schools at present is the full implementation of the requirements of Northern Ireland Curriculum Mathematics. In what we have said earlier we do not wish to create the impression that the 1990 legislation contains only a restatement of ideas from the Cockcroft Report. This is certainly not the case. For example, the programmes of study and attainment targets require pupils to work with computer packages (including databases and spreadsheets) in a way that could not have been foreseen easily by a committee of inquiry carrying out its deliberations in the 1978-82 period. Nor do we wish to give the impression that nothing of much significance happened in mathematical education prior to the Cockcroft Report. As Cornelius (1985) observed: *'When it appeared, in January 1982, the Cockcroft Report said what many people had been saying for a long time.'*

The report itself acknowledged that many of its recommendations had been made before in official reports and professional publications. In 1977 Alastair McIntosh, later to be a member of the Cockcroft committee, made the following observation in an article surveying past official reports on mathematics teaching:

Sixty to one hundred years ago, steps for the improvement of primary mathematics were being advocated. They included

1. *Don't start formal work too early.*
2. *Use materials and start from practical activities.*
3. *Give children problems and freedom initially to find their own methods of solution.*
4. *Children must have particular problems from which to generalise.*
5. *Go for relevance and the involvement of the child.*
6. *Go for reasons and understanding of processes. Never give mechanical rules.*
7. *Emphasise and encourage discussion by children.*
8. *Follow understanding with practice and applications.*

It is doubtful if one child in a million has received a mathematical education consistently following these principles at every stage. (McIntosh 1977)

With the enactment of Northern Ireland Curriculum Mathematics (and corresponding legislation in England and Wales) it is now law that one million children in a million should receive such a mathematical education.

PROBLEM SOLVING

A STAFF WORKSHOP

1. Which problem solving strategies would you use to solve these problems?

2. What age group could attempt these problems?

3. Can the problems be adapted by presentation to suit different age and ability groups?

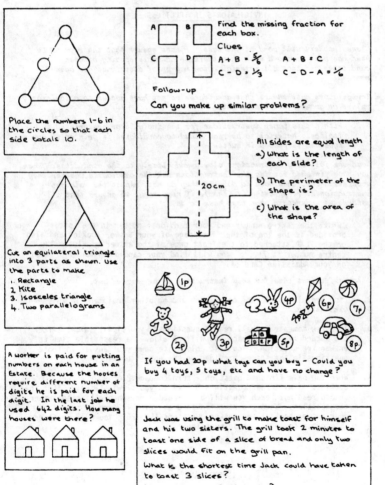

Place the numbers 1-6 in the circles so that each side totals 10.

Find the missing fraction for each box.

Clues

A + B = $\frac{5}{6}$ A + B = C

C - D = $\frac{1}{3}$ C - D - A = $\frac{1}{6}$

Follow-up

Can you make up similar problems?

All sides are equal length

a) What is the length of each side?

b) The perimeter of the shape is?

c) What is the area of the shape?

20cm

Cut an equilateral triangle into 3 parts as shown. Use the parts to make

1. Rectangle
2. Kite
3. Isosceles triangle
4. Two parallelograms

If you had 20p what toys can you buy — Could you buy 4 toys, 5 toys, etc and have no change?

A worker is paid for putting numbers on each house in an Estate. Because the houses require different number of digits he is paid for each digit. In the last job he used 642 digits. How many houses were there?

Jack was using the grill to make toast for himself and his two sisters. The grill took 2 minutes to toast one side of a slice of bread and only two slices would fit on the grill pan.

What is the shortest time Jack could have taken to toast 3 slices?

What about 4, 5 slices etc?

NORTHERN IRELAND SCHOOLS EXAMINATIONS COUNCIL

GCSE EXAMINATIONS

MATHEMATICS

AURAL AND COMPUTATION TEST

INTERMEDIATE LEVEL

[26-81]

INVIGILATOR'S INSTRUCTIONS

Class teachers will conduct the test. Please ensure that the room to be used has been arranged such that there is adequate spacing between candidates and that all material which may be of assistance has been removed.

Invigilators must ensure that candidates do not have access to calculators, rulers or geometrical instruments.

N.B. Within this paper instructions for the invigilator are printed in Italics. Material to be read aloud to candidates is printed in Roman type and is placed in quotes - ' '.

Read the following instructions slowly and clearly to the candidates. When you have finished reading the instructions ask the candidates whether they understand what they have to do. If they do not, repeat the relevant instruction(s) re-phrasing it (them), if necessary, to ensure that all candidates understand what they have to do.

1. 'Write the centre number and your candidate number in the spaces provided at the top of the first page of your answer booklet and also on the FLAP attached to the front page of the answer booklet. The centre number is 71.... You will find your candidate number printed on your Admission Card'.

Allow sufficient time for this instruction to be carried out.

2. 'You are allowed to use only a pen and no other equipment in this examination.

3. In a few moments I shall read 7 questions to you slowly twice. After the second reading of each you will be allowed a reasonable time to answer the question. You must only write down your answer to those questions in the spaces provided on the answer booklet.

4. When you have finished question 7 turn to page 2 of your answer booklet. I will read questions 8 - 14 to you slowly twice. After the second reading of each you will be allowed a reasonable time to answer the question. When you have finished question 14 turn to page 4 of your answer booklet and answer questions 15 - 20. You will be given 15 minutes to answer these questions'.

(Summer 1989)

When you have read these instructions to the candidates check that they have been fully understood before proceeding with the test.

For each of the questions 1 - 14 inclusive allow up to 1 minute for each question, including the reading time for the question. If it is obvious that all candidates have arrived at their answers within this time, proceed to the next question.

Begin the test by stating:

'Here is the first question. Remember, you must <u>only</u> write down the <u>answers</u> for questions 1 to 7. Listen carefully.

1. A stamp costs 18 pence. How much would 20 stamps cost?

2. Twenty small oranges cost 80 pence. What is the price of one?

3. A tyre for a bicycle costs £6.50. I buy two. How much change do I get from £20?

4. In a test Ruth got 30 marks out of 40. What was her percentage mark?

5. A classroom is 12.5 m long and 7.5 m wide. What is the perimeter of the room?

6. The area of a square is 68 square centimetres. What is the approximate length of one side?

7. What is the smallest number that 3, 5, and 10 will all divide into?

Now turn to page 2 of your answer booklet. As I read each of questions 8 to 14 to you, study the printed material beside the question number and write your answer in the space provided in the booklet. You may make notes on the paper if you find this useful. Here is question 8.

8. How far is it from Barnstaple to Carmarthen?

9. Which country has the highest standard of living?

10. What is the difference between the maximum temperature in May and the minimum temperature in January?

11. What is the estimated 10-year return for a man aged 42 paying £80 per month?

12. How long would it take to roast six pounds of pork at the higher temperature?

13. Which exercise would use up 425 kilojoules in a quarter of an hour?

14. This beaker contains 75 millilitres of liquid. How many millilitres would it contain if it were filled up to the full mark?

Stop writing. Now turn to page 4 of your answer booklet. You have 15 minutes starting from now to attempt questions 15 to 20.'

INTERMEDIATE

NORTHERN IRELAND SCHOOLS EXAMINATIONS COUNCIL

Centre Number

71

Candidate Number

General Certificate of Secondary Education

Summer 1989

MATHEMATICS

Aural and Computation Test
(Intermediate Level)

[26—8]

Time allowed: 30 minutes

FRIDAY 12 MAY, AFTERNOON

CANDIDATE'S ANSWER BOOKLET

Write your Centre number and Candidate number in the spaces provided above and on the flap attached to the **Front Page** of this Booklet. The Invigilator will tell you your Centre number. Your candidate number is printed on your Admission Card.

Do not open the Answer Booklet until you are told to do so. Listen carefully to the instructions given to you by the Invigilator. If you do not understand any of them ask the Invigilator to repeat or explain them to you.

You are allowed to use only a pen and no other equipment in this examination.

Answers to questions 1–7

1. £_____

2. _____p

3. £_____

4. _____%

5. _____m

6. _____cm

7. _____

**For Examiner's
use only**

Total Marks

TE&S 89/11 4/4 14000
© N. Ireland S.E.C. 1989

8. Distances (miles)

Aberdeen
Aberystwyth
Barnstaple
Birmingham
Brighton
Bristol
Cambridge
Cardiff
Carlisle
Carmarthen

```
472
602  212
430  119  176
604  268  202  177
511  126   98   85  151
468  221  250  101  119  154
532  115  137  107  186   45  189
234  235  367  194  365  275  256  295
522   48  200  133  249  108  233   67  284
```

Answer_____ miles

9.

STANDARD OF LIVING

NUMBER PER 100 HOUSEHOLDS	CARS	FRIDGES	VACUUM CLEANERS	WASHING MACHINES
GERMANY	60	88	89	66
FRANCE	53	73	40	51
BRITAIN	45	60	84	63

Answer_____

10.

		Jan	Feb	Mar	Apr	May	Jun
Innsbruck	Max °C	2	4	11	15	21	23
(Austria)	Min °C	−6	−4	0	3	8	11

Answer_____ °C

11.

	Your Estimated 10-Year Return		
Male Age At Entry	Paying £10 per month	Paying £20 per month	Paying £30 per month
20–34	£2,552	£5,104	£7,656
35–39	£2,542	£5,084	£7,626
40–54	£2,504	£5,008	£7,512
55–59	£2,408	£4,816	£7,224
60–64	£2,350	£4,700	£7,050

Women will receive benefits equal to a man who is four years younger.

Answer £_____

12.

		Low Mark 3 Gas/325°F Electric	High Mark 7 Gas/425°F Electric
	Beef	25 mins. lb plus 25 mins.	15 mins. lb plus 20 mins.
	Lamb	20–25 mins. lb plus 25 mins.	20 mins. lb plus 20 mins.
Roasting Chart	Veal	35 mins. lb plus 35 mins.	25 mins. lb plus 25 mins.
	Pork	35 mins. lb plus 35 mins.	30 mins. lb plus 30 mins.
	Chicken	20 mins. lb plus 20 mins.	20 mins. lb
	Duck	25 mins. lb plus 20 mins.	20 mins. lb
	Turkey	below 10 lbs 25 mins. lb above 10 lbs 18 mins. lb	below 10 lbs 22 mins. lb above 10 lbs 15 mins. lb

Answer_____

13. *Exercise for 30 minutes*   *Energy*
                                       kilojoules

Slow walking	400
Brisk walking	650
Jogging	1000
Badminton or dancing	650
Squash	1000
Swimming	850
Watching TV	200

Answer_____

14.

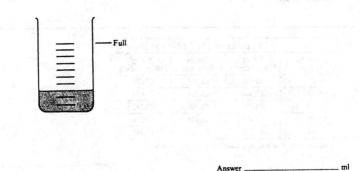
Full

Answer _____ ml

3   [Turn over

Answer the following six questions which will probably need some written calculations. You should show your calculations neatly in the space below. You have fifteen minutes to answer the questions.

15. Find the mean of 4196, 23, 107.   Answer_____

16. Divide 15.6 by 1.2.   Answer_____

17. Find the value of three eighths of £256.   Answer £_____

18. Find the area of a square of side 9.7 cm.   Answer_____ cm²

19. List the prime factors of 182.   Answer_____

20. Find the total number of days from 26th January 1989 to 30th April 1989 inclusive.

                    Answer_____ days

COMMON SCIENCE

Barbara Erwin

The car boot slammed shut with a rattle of keys as Madeline collected her box of materials for the day's lessons, and she made her way towards the school with a large basket full of books and worksheets on one arm, handbag slung over one shoulder and the large box in both hands. She was met excitedly by a group of youngsters at the door. They were in the P6 class she had been taking yesterday for science. "Miss, Miss", they excitedly hissed as they crowded round to help her into the school. "We've found out how to make it float." Madeline smiled at them pleased that they had become so involved with the science she had been doing yesterday. She had set them homework to try out something they did not have time for in class and had hoped that they would take it away and try it out at home with their parents. Some children obviously had been successful and she hoped that this enthusiasm would spread beyond the school gates. Parents were very wary of many new initiatives especially if it was felt to distract from the urgency of preparing pupils for the all important Eleven+ examination, and science had been seen in the past as yet another of these distractions. Yet these were P6 pupils and they had only just started to study science. As science coordinator she was seen as an expert and her expertise was being used to try to give other teachers some idea of how to go about teaching science. Madeline's obvious enthusiasm was beginning to pay off with both pupils and some of the staff who were attempting to follow up the work after her weekly visit. Other areas of the curriculum were being explored and a lot of interesting work was being generated following from the work in science. So the pupils are learning something about the principles of floating and sinking she thought, smiling to herself as she walked down the corridor to her classroom.

INTRODUCTION

This chapter reflects on science education in Northern Ireland. Curriculum development in science has to some extent been reflected in the major curriculum initiatives that have taken place over the past two decades which have emanated from England and Wales. Some interesting data were collected by the APU programme and much of this is still influential in preparations for change that will be required if the Common Curriculum is to be successfully implemented in Northern Ireland schools. The implications of GCSE and the Secondary Science Curriculum Review (SSCR) in secondary schools together with the effect of Primary Guidelines (NICED , 1986) are also to be considered to be important. The impact of the common curriculum for schools, teachers and pupils will also be discussed in the light of current good practice.

PRIMARY SCIENCE

The success of any edifice depends on its foundations and the implementation of a successful science curriculum will depend on the groundwork prepared in our primary schools. Many primary teachers do not consider themselves to be qualified to teach science. Most primary teachers are women who acquired very little science during their schooling . They quite understandably feel very uneasy about the present trends to the emphasis on science and technology. Indeed, until the implementation of the Common Curriculum, much successful work in classrooms, which has prepared pupils for their secondary school careers and pleased parents, has not included science at all. It is this group of teachers within the profession who need additional support, training, and encouragement if the future success of our children in science is to be ensured. The responses of many are exemplified by one teacher who, during an In-service course was presented with a copy of the programmes of study for key stage 2. He felt so overwhelmed by the amount of material to be included, by the unfamiliar territory and by his own lack of experience that he reverted to a mere counting exercise. As the end of the discussion he exclaimed loudly, 'There are twenty nine 'shoulds' in that programme of study. How on earth would I cover them all?'

Science education in primary schools has seen some innovative developments over the past two centuries. It is interesting to note from inventories of the national schools in the mid 1800s that some science equipment featured and that nature study was common. In the present century in primary schools it would not be an unfair generalisation to note that, until the past decade, no significant advance on 'nature study' has taken place. Where there was anything approaching a broad and balanced curriculum in science it was usually as a result of a particular teacher's enthusiasm and not as a result of a specific school policy. Individual pupils may therefore have had an intermittent and patchy experience of science throughout their primary career. It was common for science to be theoretical, or based on the biological aspects with the occasional spectacular event such as dissecting bulls' eyes. It was not therefore surprising for secondary schools to assume that pupils had no previous science education and to organise their science programmes accordingly.

Much of the innovative work in schools in the early 1970s failed to have the impact justified by the work involved in writing the materials. This largely resulted from very 'teacher unfriendly' materials that were hard to access. Nevertheless, the resulting classroom materials *Learning through Science* formed a sound foundation for much of the later science developments that are an invaluable resource today.

Primary Science was given great encouragement in the early 1980s by the Department of Education for Northern Ireland when grants enabled teachers to attend one year full-time courses run initially at Stranmillis College and later at St. Mary's College. Many teachers who attended these courses went back into their own schools and attempted to organise a science programme throughout the school. Nevertheless the impact of this initiative was not as cost effective as had been hoped. This was not because of the nature of the courses or the quality of the people involved, but more as a result of an unfavourable climate in schools. The value of the teachers' expertise has more recently been recognised, and many of them have been seconded to field officer and curriculum support posts with the Education and Library Boards in Northern Ireland.

The primary guidelines initiative failed to stimulate the development of science programmes in most schools. The science document was very helpful and many ideas have been subsumed into the Proposals for the Science Curriculum (DENI, 1989). What mitigated against the impact of the document was the timing of its publication. NICED had published the primary guidelines over a fairly lengthy period and science had been preceded by Health Education, literacy and numeracy. Many primary schools were making significant progress in other areas of the curriculum and simply had not had time to deal with science. However the Science Guideline is a valuable resource to support present developments. The experience that many schools acquired as a result of primary guidelines work in sharing ideas and holding meaningful curriculum meetings, in working with and through co-ordinators and in disseminating good practice within their institutions will prove useful in the immediate future.

SECONDARY SCIENCE

For the first time in British education, following the Education Reform Act (1988) all pupils are now guaranteed the opportunity of a systematic, progressive science curriculum from their first weeks in primary school until the end of compulsory schooling at 16. Moreover the science curriculum will be broad and balanced ranging across both biological and the physical sciences. For pupils the exciting development is the opportunity for exploration and investigation in science. This means all pupils having access to practical experiences. Gone are the days of laboriously copying complicated diagrams from chalkboards and the presumption by the teacher that this will be adequate. Science will be active, involve problem-solving and be experiential and related to the personal and social lives of the pupils. The commitment to and enthusiasm for this type of science within the Science Working Groups both in England and Wales and in Northern Ireland had arisen from opportunities to be involved in and observe good practice both in primary and secondary schools. However the impact of GCSE and the work of the Secondary Science Curriculum Review (SSCR) can be seen to have had a profound influence on the curriculum.

Many teachers of science both at primary and secondary level belong to the Association for Science Education (ASE). The ASE was instrumental in having the Secondary Science Curriculum Review

(SSCR) set up in 1982. Within Northern Ireland the work of SSCR was supported by DENI, the Education and Library Boards and the Northern Ireland Council for Educational Development (NICED). The philosophy of the Review was that of an 'aims into practice' model (Caul 1990) of curriculum development in which teachers identified their problems, interests and enthusiasms and worked in groups to develop answers, solve problems and develop curriculum materials. This contrasted with many previous attempts which were all dominated by central agencies in which 'experts' prepared material for dissemination, often under the aegis of the Schools' Council. The lack of ownership of the ideas and minimal involvement by practising teachers meant that many good ideas simply gathered dust.

The learning theory that underpinned the approach was the 'constructivist view of learning', promoted by the Children's Learning in Science Project, based in the University of Leeds. The view that pupils are empty vessels into which knowledge is poured was discarded. Instead the working groups were asked to consider the need for pupils to become actively involved in their learning in order to construct meaning and make sense of information and experiences for themselves. Teachers were also reminded that pupils came to science with a vast experience of the world and with their own explanations of how things worked. These 'pupil views' of science are often quite different from 'scientists views' of scientific phenomena and are resistant to modification. SSCR considered that much of the failure of school science had resulted from a failure to interest pupils, particularly girls and to challenge their preconceived views of science.

Over the past five years a great deal of curriculum development has been 'assessment led'. For the secondary school teacher perhaps the most novel features of the syllabi were the explicit statements of objectives, and the discrimination between knowledge and processes or skills in science. There was an underlying assumption that differentiation would operate within the classroom and laboratory so that all pupils would be able to show what they *know, understand and can do*, although this has been slow to have been put into practice in science. Many useful lessons have been learned that will help to improve the quality of assessment in the common curriculum at all levels from key stage 1 to 4.

The success of GCSE in promoting true investigation skills and in helping students to become more self confident in the laboratory as well as during fieldwork was bought at a price. The professionalism of so many teachers committed to making science work for their pupils resulted in many new pressures for additional preparation and planning. Important lessons must be learned for the future assessment arrangements. In Northern Ireland NISEC, as it was then, offered training programmes. For those who ran them it proved a difficult exercise because of the number of unanswered questions. There is clearly a need to establish clear guidelines that are not ambiguous and inspire confidence in teachers so that their assessment procedures equate with colleagues in other schools, is important. It is gratifying to learn from NISEAC that our assessment procedures do not have to equate exactly with those from England and Wales, and that the teacher is to be central to the whole assessment process.

THE COMMON CURRICULUM AND SCIENCE

The Science Working Group in Northern Ireland had the benefit of having access to the report of the English and Welsh Working Party and to the non-statutory guidance materials produced for the National Curriculum Council. In many respects it made the task easier and its report is considered to contain considerable advances, particularly regarding attainment target 1 : Exploring and Investigating in Science. The document did not pretend to present anything that was in itself original, but to render a distillation of good practice in primary and secondary schools. Except for one attainment target comprising mostly material of a geological nature, the vast majority of the Working Party Report has now become statutory.

It is important to re-emphasise several important points. It must always be borne in mind that exploration and investigation are at the centre of all good science teaching. It will not therefore be enough for teachers to go through the list of attainment targets and statements of attainment and teach the information theoretically. The proposals make this clear;

Science is both an established and expanding body of knowledge and an important way of looking at the world.......... it is by no means the only way of looking at human experience and the world. A Scientific way of working involves:
> *•responding with interest and enthusiasm*
> *•asking questions*
> *•accessing and understanding*
> *•conducting scientific investigations*
> *•appreciating ....perspectives.*

This way of delivering the science curriculum will involve large amounts of practical work and it is likely that this is what is giving cause for most concern. This occurs particularly at the lower end of many secondary schools as well as in primary schools.

The concept of differentiation at GCSE caused some consternation among educationists and a great deal of effort went into trying to establish how it could be translated into the preparation of differentiated work for pupils of varying abilities. When classes contained pupils of varying abilities, it was considered unreasonable that the content and pace of teaching was pitched at only the better groups, so that those lower attainers continually struggled along, perpetually failing and losing the last remnants of their self esteem. Biology teachers became skilled at taking published practical work from standard text books and adapting it and this resulted in the publication of a handbook of practicals, *The Northern Ireland GCSE Resource Book for Biology* (Erwin 1987)

It is vital to appreciate that the common curriculum builds differentiation into the system from the age of four right up to sixteen. Hence although each of the four key stages has specific programmes of study, the key stages must operate for overlapping levels. Teachers receiving progressively older pupils in both primary and secondary schools, will need to learn to cope with an increasing array of achievement levels and abilities. It would appear that the only way out of this dilemma is an exploration of the strategies that can be employed to teach through group work at all levels. When this was suggested at Inset training sessions and GCSE Moderation meetings, some secondary teachers refused to believe it was possible. Others were concerned about the safety aspects of having different groups of pupils doing different practical activities. Another objection concerned the psychological effect this would have on lower attainers if they felt they were being given work of a simpler nature.

There are also problems facing teachers within primary schools, many of whom pride themselves on being able to teach pupils in groups. In many classrooms pupils are sorted into groups according to reading ability, and teachers listen to each pupils read every day, recording diligently how they are progressing. This is not 'group work' of the type that will be required to achieve different levels within the science curriculum. A great deal of science cannot be done without the true co-operation of a small team, both at the research level as well as at the key stage 1 . Even putting a cover on a jam jar is more easily done if one child holds the jar and material and the other one puts on the elastic band. The mere fact that children grouped at tables does not mean that they are co-operating in groups and it is a common experience of advisers and inspectors to find pupils working completely independently of each other in such situations. Managing group work and providing each child with the opportunities to acquire the necessary social skills must start from the first years in school. Structured play provides good opportunities to establish such routines and gives appropriate exploratory activities in science.

As pupils progress through the primary school they will diverge in achievement levels in science as well as other subjects. This has always been the case, but when transfer to secondary schools takes place, most secondary schools are concerned only with a pupil's abilities in Mathematics and English. Frequently pupils are streamed according to the results of standardised tests given within the first few weeks of arrival in their new school. In future it will no longer be possible to ignore a pupil's level of attainment in science. This problem poses a dilemma for both primary head-teachers and secondary schools. As it is, some primary head-teachers feel that the transfer reports that they now prepare for each pupil are ignored. Many secondary schools that have a large intake do not consider that they have enough time to deal with the information supplied and feel that a 'clean slate' approach is more advantageous to pupils.

The problem of primary-secondary liaison has been long recognised as an issue facing teachers. The problem applies not only to science, but to other subjects as they come on stream. Some secondary schools are making valiant efforts to bridge the gap by sending staff to talk to each of the feeder primary schools and many secondary schools invite pupils to visit them during their last term in primary schools. These foundations will need to be reinforced and built upon. The first group of pupils to which this problem applies is the P5 group starting the Common Curriculum in September 1990. They will enter secondary schools with three years of science experience, having achieved a range of levels. It will be interesting to see what strategies secondary schools adopt to ensure that a pupil's true abilities and achievements are recognised.

THE PRESENT STATE OF THE ART

Good practice abounds in schools throughout Northern Ireland although it is not yet uniformly distributed through the province. As a parent it is my regret that my own children have missed many experiences that are embodied in the proposals, but I look forward to seeing many children have the opportunity to start to enjoy science from their first few weeks in school.

Science has presented a bad image to many people and the responsibility for that lies at the door of the scientific community, and science teachers specifically. This explains why so many of the present teaching force gave up science as early as possible, because they considered it to be difficult, boring, exceptionally mathematical and frequently irrelevant to their own lives. The need to change these attitudes prompted those setting the GCSE criteria to allocate 15% of assessment to the personal, social and technological aspects of science. Syllabi were written to contain less theoretical information and more relevant information that related to society and its problems. Unless we nurture the attitude that science is fun, is interesting and is relevant, young people will continue to turn their backs on it.

If your personal experience of science at school consisted of little more than drawing the ubiquitous bunsen burner and copying tedious recipes from chalkboards, or learning innumerable seemingly Latin names, you may be sceptical. However my conviction that 'science is fun' comes from many hours of enjoyment at the kitchen table with my own children. They were used as the inevitable guinea pigs to try out science activities when 'I could not get my hands on other people's children!' If you have ever had the chance to listen quietly at the back of a classroom when pupils are being given opportunities to explore and investigate some aspect of science like separating the pigments in felt tip pens- that to them becomes wonderful and has a magical quality, you cannot fail to be convinced of its value. It is even more interesting to organise an evening of science fun for parents who want to know what primary science is all about. Of course science cannot always be done easily with folded arms and thick winter coats, and seeing parents stand on chairs, get down on their knees and ask questions with interest and amazement is quite an experience.

Interactive science centres are not common in this part of the world. However an excellent example of such a centre is the Ontario Science Centre, Canada. The big 'children' as well as the little ones are fascinated and amazed, and queues quickly build up to try out things. The very frustrating part is the inevitable failure of some piece of machinery to work because so many small and not so small hands have tried it out. North American and Canadian parents are very quick to support their children's love of science and the Science Centre has several invaluable publications. The Ulster Museum science bus is proving popular in the greater Belfast area and I look forward to the growth of this type of support and leisure activity to encourage young scientists.

But what of the classroom? What are these examples of good practice? Like many a giant oak, success grows from very small beginnings nurtured in the favourable soil of a supportive school. In the past we have had to convince Principals that science would enhance a child's learning experiences, for it is only when principals fully support their staff in an active manner by providing time, resources and personal reassurance that success has spread throughout the school.

The implications of the proposals have been clearly spelt out in the consultation paper (1989) but teachers in schools have clearly indicated through NICC that training in content, management, classroom organisational strategies and resources feature near the top of their list of priorities. The ASE in Northern Ireland has clarified the danger and difficulty of attempting to do practical work in classrooms that are too full of children, and where there are no suitable storage facilities for equipment. However the argument that it is a paucity of science equipment that is holding back progress is false. True it is difficult to teach magnetism or electricity without magnets, batteries, wires and bulbs, and schools are quickly realising what essentials comprise the 'bare necessities of life'. A great deal of the finance allocated for curriculum reform in science has had to go into putting plugs and sinks in primary classrooms - and that is only the beginning. However teachers perceive that their greatest need is training.

It is a good idea to start science with something very simple that you have tried out before, and with which you feel confident. It also makes good sense to let all the pupils do the same thing simultaneously and to control the pace at which they work by giving out information little by little. We have tended to have become hooked up on workcards, but this is not a suitable way of working for very young pupils or for pupils who are not used to doing practical work. To be met by a teacher and his ink-stained shirt after attempting the simplest of activities is enough to make us realise that pupils themselves often need to learn new ways of working and this may indeed take weeks or months.

INSET providers are often criticised when running courses for not simulating the real situation in which teachers have to collect, organise and distribute large amounts of bits and pieces for science. This is fair comment, except that the need is so great that INSET trainers must use the time to everyone's best advantage and not waste it in asking teachers to prepare and clear up. However, pupils need to be trained to collect, store, distribute and tidy up equipment and any mess that they have created. Teachers are inclined to forget that, with proper disciplined training, they have many pairs of willing hands, and pupils need to unlearn the helplessness that is so often engendered in many homes and schools.

For those who feel anxious, the science content and organisation of lessons must commence with simple, well-organised lessons in which the teacher feels in control of the situation and knows what to expect from the activity. She must also be clear about the intended learning outcomes. In other words, objectives should be clearly thought out and should be easily achievable.

Experiments with living things are useful starting points because such small invertebrate animals as worms and woodlice are easy to collect, and do not require much expensive equipment. Furthermore they make ideal classroom inhabitants because they are so undemanding and can even be placed in a locked cupboard over the weekend. When challenged to commence science study using these animals, a group of teachers recently reported that their pupils would try to squash them or stand on them. It soon became obvious that one of the most important learning outcomes from such a lesson may well be a change in attitude by the pupils, and that learning to handle living things is an important objective in itself before more 'worthy' skills such as observing, recording and hypothesising can become a priority.

Having decided to take the plunge the teacher faces a major decision, that is how to organise the pupils to allow them to have active, hands-on science experiences in which they can explore and investigate. No one method is correct and much depends on the subject, the expertise and confidence of the teacher and the previous experiences of children, to say nothing of the constraints of the space and science resources. To begin with, many teachers find that organising the whole class to work in small groups, that all carry out the same activity at the same time, is a useful starting point. Very often each group has an appointed group leader who is a good reader and assists the slower pupils. Other teachers find that the lower attainers or younger pupils in composite classes may not benefit so directly from this organisation and feel the need to supply differentiated work arising from a single type of experience.

Many lower primary teachers find structured play a useful mechanism for ensuring that young pupils receive the hands-on experience that they need for science, together with the close attention of an adult. All the activities have to be absorbing so that the excitement of the science activities are not dulled for the last groups after four or five others have tried it out, possibly after a long week. For children with special needs such as hearing impairment, or those coming from deprived home backgrounds, enrichment activities related to science concepts are important. Not only do these provide contexts for the development of basic concepts and associated language development, but they also assist young pupils to acquire the social skills that will be essential for the kind of science the Common Curriculum is trying to promote.

One of the benefits of attending a course or a cluster group is the opportunity to find out how things are going for other people. INSET providers frequently get requests for longer coffee breaks not for drinking coffee or for gossiping but for an exchange of views. This supportive aspect to curriculum development has been going on in many schools across the age range. Even those groups in which teachers are working with pupils of different abilities or age ranges find this exchange of information proves useful. Part of the armoury of teachers has to be the ability to adapt ideas and instructions to suit their pupils, because very few printed materials are entirely suitable. In fact the *Ginn* scheme (1989, 1990) does not use worksheets for infants, in common with many others. Some talented teachers are able to produce their own worksheets, either with the aid of IT or with pen and paper. We must all learn to harness such imaginative work for the benefit of all pupils in our schools and ensure that it does not lie idle. As greater numbers of teachers are seconded to write curriculum materials these talents will hopefully enhance all our work.

One of the interesting things that teachers discover about science is the hidden talents which it unlocks in their pupils. How often I have been swept into a classroom to see a piece of work that the reluctant writer has produced as a result of the liberating experience of science. Many teachers report that the traditionally capable pupil who would have scored highly in transfer procedure tests as well as maths and spelling tests do not cope so well within the more open-ended, investigative, probem-solving science. This was particularly important in GCSE sciences, where it became obvious that very often it was the language and written instructions that became barriers to many pupils' achievement. The ability to read instructions became a prerequisite for success. However, when lower attainers understand the problem and are given the opportunities to try things out for themselves with the equipment in front of them, teachers are often astonished to see how practical and capable many pupils really are. Science will become important to many pupils as it will allow them to succeed and shine, raising their self esteem.

Perhaps one of the most exciting ways in which science becomes effective is for the whole school to become involved in a project. I visited one school recently that had taken 'Materials' as its theme for the term and each class produced attractive and interesting displays around the school. Many of these were hands-on displays and the whole project added to the general atmosphere of excitement throughout the school. The added bonus was that on Open Day, parents had a good idea of the type of activities that were going on.

Some schools take on very ambitious projects that involve not only the whole school, but also the wider community. One such project involved Cairncastle primary school and GEC Alsthom in Larne. The impetus for the project came from the curriculum support teacher for science but required the enthusiastic co-operation of all the staff in the small, three-teacher school. Not only did it involve more recognisable science activities such as the investigation of metals, forces and control technology, but it spread to involve the local history of the former aluminium factory in Larne, a play written by the pupils called 'Turbo Man' (an imaginary character built from scrap metal and batteries) and a mini enterprise project. This project concerned recycling aluminium cans, and it used the profits from the business to finance other aspects. It involved pupils working with representatives from the Ulster Bank, LEDU and the personnel department of GEC. The pupils designed a can crusher, which was made by the apprentices in GEC, to save space when packing the cans for sale to the scrap-metal merchant.

It was interesting to hear the views of those from industry who had been involved with the children and at first had felt such involvement could be a waste of time and energy. The end result was an invaluable learning experience for all concerned and it was interesting to see a school that felt confident enough to open the classroom doors to outsiders and ask them to become involved in their pupils' appreciation of science, technology, and the world of business.

Even though teachers may not feel they have the time and commitment to become involved in a large industry project, it is important for children to appreciate the links between classroom science and the world of work. Although it takes enormous effort and organisation to take pupils out of the classroom, many have found that industrial visits support their classroom work and bring fresh enthusiasm and excitement to a theme of work. Visits to farms, bakeries, lemonade factories and dairies are rich sources of ideas and most firms are very appreciative of the interest shown.

SUMMARY

The challenge of the introduction of science into the school curriculum creates new demands on teachers for relevance, interest and constant stimulation for all pupils. Teachers will need support in order to develop better ways of managing their pupils so that achievement can match expectation. Differentiated schemes of work will become a reality. Assessment will become helpful in diagnosing pupil progress as well as commending achievement. Records of progress and achievement which are to be developed must be helpful and manageable and not become so burdensome that teachers cannot cope. And finally, Science must become a stimulating vehicle for the delivery of many aspects of the curriculum, and for the delivery of the cross-curricular themes.

PROLOGUE

The hands of the clock ticked on round to the end of the lesson. The pupils had tidied up the remnants of their latest science activity. Interest was beginning to wane as the end of school approached but the youngsters were responding enthusiastically still to Madeline's questions, "Can anyone explain why the balloon over the plastic bottle shot up much quicker than the one over the glass bottle?" she queried. Most faces looked puzzled and very few hands went up, "Can no one make a guess?" Very shyly and slowly Benjamin's hand went up. He was the slowest youngster in the whole class and found writing and reading almost painful. He had been making some progress recently and his science work seemed to generate a spark of interest. Madeline found that science activities liberated the lower attaining pupils from the difficulties of language that shackled them in more traditional classroom activities, provided the tasks were presented carefully. These situations gave such pupils a chance to shine. The more able children were always reluctant to attempt an answer for fear of being wrong. "Well, Benjamin?" she asked. His reply came out clearly and unhesitatingly and there was a moment of silence. "Well, done Benjamin !!!"

THE NORTHERN IRELAND CURRICULUM FOR ENGLISH:
A HISTORICAL PERSPECTIVE

Gertrude Patterson

The National Curriculum English Working Group under the Chairmanship of Professor Brian Cox submitted its final report, *English from ages 5 to 16*, containing recommendations for the content of the English Curriculum for England and Wales, at the end of May 1989. The Northern Ireland group followed, publishing its *Proposals for the English Curriculum* in October of the same year. The Cox Report was swiftly superseded by the attainment targets and programmes of study, *English in the National Curriculum*, published by HMSO in 1990 and again the Northern Ireland equivalent followed in August of the same year. Both reports were circulated freely to schools and other appropriate education establishments and were generally welcomed with enthusiasm - and, perhaps understandably with a certain sense of relief - by teachers, for each came to represent a consensus within the profession about what constitutes (and, as many claimed, had for a long time represented) good practice within the teaching of English. Since neither report was published in the normal way and therefore neither was available in bookshops, the general public - that of course, included the parents of pupils concerned - had to rely on newspaper comment to gain access to the ideas that each contained. Inevitably, and not just because it was the first, greater interest lay in what the Cox Committee had to say and the newspaper coverage which followed this report was often misleading, wrong or even contradictory as journalists, and other non-professional commentators to summarise or encapsulate in headlines that would catch the attention of readers of the left or right, the complexities of its professionally and academically orientated argument. More seriously, perhaps, neither report is easily available to teachers and new entrants to the profession so that, for many, the programmes of study and attainment targets exist as lists of separate tasks and activities to be undertaken at the different stages of a pupil's development, unexplained by the rationale that is at their foundation, knowledge of which is crucial, not just to a full understanding of their meaning but more importantly, perhaps, to implement them in the interrelated way in which their originators intended. Professor Cox makes similar points in justification of his book *Cox on Cox* (1991) which sets out to redefine and elaborate the vision of English on which the National Curriculum requirements are based. In so doing, he aims to provide an important resource for teachers and an informative guide to parents and all those with a professional interest in the teaching of the subject. What follows here is a more modest attempt to provide a similar explanation for the Northern Ireland Curriculum.

Chronologically the successor to the Cox Report, the Northern Ireland Report, *Proposals for the English Curriculum*, has to be read within the context of the earlier 'parent' document. Both, however, need to be set within the wider historical perspective of the period of debate about English teaching and what constitutes competence in the subject that preceded them, for it is an awareness of this important backdrop that provides a fuller understanding, both about what is new and not new in the conditions that culminated in an attempt to provide a common curriculum for schools, and about what is new and not new in the curriculum itself. The 'new' is, of course, often mistakenly confused in today's debates on educational matters with the 'progressive', the 'liberal' or the 'trendy', depending on the vantage point, political or otherwise, from which the practice of teaching is viewed, while what is not new is correspondingly assumed to be 'traditional', 'conservative' or 'old-fashioned'. What is unequivocally not new, however, is that the history of English teaching shows that curriculum change has always come about as a result of claims made about 'falling standards'.

The last two decades were marked by several important documents on the teaching of English, the most significant of which were the Bullock Report, A Language for Life, published in 1975 and the *Report of the Committee of Enquiry into the Teaching of English Language* under Sir John Kingman, in March 1988. The first was set up in the aftermath of the famous Black Papers of 1969 and 1970, which were strongly critical of the 'progressive' teaching methods of the 1960s and as a result of a National Foundation of Educational Research publication *Trends in Reading Standards* in 1972, which expressed concern about the reading abilities of some 11- and 15-year olds. The Secretary of State for the day, Margaret Thatcher, set up a committee of inquiry under Sir Alan Bullock, and charged it with the specific task of investigating claims made by Start and Wells in the NFER publication about falling standards in reading. The Bullock committee extended its remit considerably, however, and the report that followed was a comprehensive survey of English teaching at both primary and secondary levels that made more than three hundred recommendations about how the subject should be taught, some relating specifically to how teachers themselves should be educated in order to fulfil them. The Kingman Report had a similar embryology, again brought to birth as a result to concern about falling standards, this time identified as *observable deficiencies* in pupils' use of language, articulated in HMI Reports of the Department of Education and Science in 1978 and 1979 and in response to a concern for greater coherence and consistency in the quality of English curriculum provided by schools, expressed in a Government White Paper *Better Schools* in 1984, presented by the Secretary of State, Sir Keith Joseph. In the same year, Her Majesty's Inspectorate initiated their proposals for a coherent English curriculum in an important and controversial booklet (1984), which provoked such outraged concern among teachers that it was reprinted with the responses of the profession contained in an Appendix, in a new version in 1986. Criticism of the initial publication arose from what teachers perceived to be the threat of return to the 'old-fashioned' ways of the forties and fifties, in the proposal made that pupils should be taught about language, which they perceived to be explicit teaching and practice of the old Latinate rules of grammar, with regular rituals imposed of parsing and general analysis, which were outside the educational experience of many young teachers. It was out of the confusion of this mistrust and misunderstanding that the Kingman committee was set up to look specifically at the needs of teachers and to make recommendations about the knowledge of language that they required in order to ensure that their pupils might make more explicit progress in the acquisition of language skills than some had perceived to have been the case in the 'progressive' and 'trendy' sixties.

The Report of the Kingman Committee was published in 1988 and, while not required to comment specifically on the English curriculum itself, it too, like Bullock, extended its remit somewhat to provide illustration of how teachers' increased knowledge about language might be integrated into classroom practice. Response to Kingman Report was, not surprisingly, mixed. For those who wanted to see a return to traditional grammar teaching, it was disappointingly non-prescriptive in its approach to language. Indeed the comment made in the introductory pages seemed to confirm that there was little hope for the 'progress' that they had anticipated when the Chairman of the committee was ready to acknowledge the inadequacies of *old-fashioned grammar teaching and learning by rote*:

We have been impressed by the evidence we have received that this gave an inadequate account of the English language by treating it virtually as a branch of Latin, and constructing a rigid descriptive code rather than a dynamic description of language in use. It was also ineffective as a means of developing a command of English in all its manifestations. (Kingman 1988, 3, para 1:11)

For others, the proposed 'model', underwritten by the insistence that *'since all pupils are entitled to an education that will equip them to use the English language to the best of their abilities, all teachers need some explicit knowledge of the forms and uses of the English language'*, marked a step backwards not forwards, particularly when Kingman went on to propose some targets for the knowledge, skills and understanding they might be expected to display at various educational stages, together with implications for the assessment of these. (Kingman 1988 4-5) And so it was out of the heat of the debate that followed the Kingman Report, conducted both among journalists and among politicians of the right and the left, that Professor Brian Cox (himself editor of an contributor to the famous Black Papers of 1969-70) was asked to chair a working group to prepare proposals for English in the National Curriculum that would 'build on' the work of the Kingman Committee, as it was in the aftermath of both Kingman and Cox that the Northern Ireland Working Party, chaared by Geraldine Pettigrew, Head of a Department of English in a Belfast school, was charged with producing comparable proposals for English in Northern Ireland. Given the fact that English teaching had, for the first time for many years, come into the foreground of political debate, and that Professor Cox's Working Group was chosen carefully by the Education Secretary of the day, Kenneth Baker, to point the way more clearly in the direction of a more conservative and traditional approach to the subject than Kingman had done, it is little wonder that the Cox Report was awaited by all concerned with great interest. Each committee had, of course, to take account of the well-worn path of research findings on the subject that had preceded them in coming up with proposals that would provide the right curriculum for the nineties.

One of the problems of the Kingman Report for the ultra-conservative and traditionalists was that, like his predecessor, Sir Alan Bullock, Kingman failed to confirm the concerns about falling standards which had brought both committees so urgently into being. Nor had the conclusions of the Assessment of performance Unit, set up in response on this occasion, to the Labour Prime Minister's concern in his 1976 Ruskin College lecture about 'falling standards' in the nation's schools, which failed to take account of pupils' 'real needs' by providing a curriculum that was too academic in its reverence for the great tradition of English Literature and hence irrelevant to the world of work which pupils had to be prepared for. Both the APU, in its assessment and monitoring of the language achievement of 11+ and 15+ year olds in schools, and Bullock to assert stubbornly refused to catalogue the failures of schools in the collapse of literacy and the need to return to the good-old fashioned ways of rote learning and grammar-grind as the only means of addressing the problems. Bullock sensibly urged caution in making too-easy assumptions in diagnosing and remedying the perceived illnesses of schools. In the opening pages of his report he writes:

It is extremely difficult to say whether or not standards of spoken or written English have fallen. There is no convincing evidence available and most opinions depend largely on subjective impressions. (Bullock 1975 6).

Though he stated as well that such opinions should not be dismissed out of hand, the introduction to his report indicates the invalidity of making comparisons with the past in attempting to assess linguistic competence in the present. For example, could it be said that the language demands made on 16-year olds in the seventies (and we could add, the eighties and nineties) - a period of increased educational provision when more and more children from wider and wider social bands stayed on in schools to take CSE and GCE English - could properly be compared with those made on a much narrower sample of the school population of the thirties and forties? Could the language tasks be compared? As an alternative to measuring the present with the past in order to define 'standards', Bullock, like Kingman, attempted instead to analyse the nature and purpose of English as a school subject the complexities of the tasks facing teachers of English and those designing a curriculum for English for pupils of mixed ability (and now, of course, increasingly, mixed race), which took account of the range and variety of English in which pupils need to be competent in confronting the needs of coping with contemporary society - not just the world of work but a world of expanding and changing higher education and vocational training to which increasing numbers sought and are still seeking entry. Bullock met the challenge in fulfilling the remit that his committee defined for itself in 1975 not just in its 333 proposals about the teaching of English in primary and secondary schools but also in including recommendations about how teachers themselves needed to be educated. The APU made fewer but no less positive statements in the planning and assessment of English. The Kingman Inquiry resulted in 18 proposals referring specifically (though not exclusively) to the training of teachers. All were concerned not just to refute adverse criticism by defending the best they had found in the current practice of their day, but to go on to assert that it was a continuous aim within this practice to find ways of raising standards, by acknowledging the fact that, since the uses to which the skills of English are applied do not remain constant in a society that is changing, it follows that English teachers have to take account of such change in offering a curriculum capable of adapting to new demands. There is, of course, a difference between acknowledging the need for a flexible curriculum and giving in to vagueness by asserting instead the diffuse nature of the subject, as Bullock readily admitted. Confronting the question 'What is English?' - the same question which Cox and the Northern Ireland committee had also to confront in defining their rationale - Bullock stated that, unlike other areas of the curriculum, it is not a body of knowledge that can be identified, quantified and transmitted. In terms closely reminiscent of John Dixon (1967), Bullock identified three sets of attitudes to the subject in the schools surveyed by his committee, though, in the carefully balanced voice that characterises the report as a whole, he cautions his audience against assuming that any one of these predominates in any one single particular school practice. It is worthwhile looking more closely at these, in order more fully to understand the foundations on which much of the new curriculum for English is built.

The first approach identified by Bullock was consistent with the practice of English teaching in the twenties and thirties, and is marked by its attempt to draw in the boundaries of the subject by defining English skills narrowly in terms of certain formal requirements, its principle being that deliberate practice of grammatical and other controllable tasks through text-book exercises would provide the essential kit needed to approach the wider world of learning and living. The second approach was that which John Dixon himself initially put forward as his own preferred model for the teaching of English as a result of the Dartmouth Seminar on the subject in 1965: this is known as the 'personal growth' approach to language development in which the individual child is perceived to be the centre of the learning process, the chief aim of which is to promote a personal and individualised view of the world. The third, described by Bullock, was marked by a rejection of what John Dixon had called the 'cultural heritage' model of English: the view, as popularly understood, that English is essentially about transmitting and fostering appreciation of the 'best' in the 'Great Tradition' of English literature. This was the element added to the initial literacy or 'skills' model of the twenties and the thirties by those nurtured in the classical tradition - on the assumption no child should leave school without knowing something about Shakespeare, Chaucer and the 'Greats', whatever the ultimate destination of pupils in the world of work. Instead, Bullock found an emphasis that identified English as a potent instrument for social change. For them, English was about developing social awareness and responsibility by confronting social issues within the curriculum. The goal of bridging social gaps in the sharing of a common cultural heritage was unacceptable, not just because it was unrealistic but because within it was the notion of the superiority of a middle-class culture. Bullock was careful to point out the dangers of oversimplification in describing these approaches as if there were factions within the profession who blazoned such ideas as political manifestos. What he was identifying, however, were emphases within the wide spectrum of practice that characterised teaching in the schools he surveyed.

It is easy, of course, to find echoes of all of these approaches persisting in the concerns, anxieties and prejudices of all those participating in the heated debate that still rages even after the National Curriculum has been set in place - from the pleas on behalf of Shakespeare made by Prince Charles, for example, who fears that the Great Tradition is being lost in the utilitarian culture of present-day Britain, to the more serious indictment of teacher training made in government pronouncements about Colleges and Departments of Education who are allegedly not preparing students for the real work of the classroom but filling their heads instead with left-wing theories of education. There are, of course, obvious weaknesses in adopting single mindedly any of the three approaches outlined by Bullock in the 1970s. The weakness of the first is evidenced in the continuing research referred to both by Bullock and Kingman (in the passage already quoted) that there was no merit in teaching the skills of English divorced from the real acts of communication and comprehension that were the actual language needs of pupils. Reiterated by Kingman thirteen years later in his shorter survey, it was this confident assertion that displeased a government anxious for quick-fix remedies to the ills of education in English rather than comprehensive analyses of the problems involved.

The weaknesses of the other two approaches are equally evident to those responsible for to writing proposals in the new curriculum, as they were to Bullock and indeed as they were also to John Dixon himself when he came to review his perceptions of English in *Growth Through English* (1975). In overcoming the weakness of the 'personal growth' approach, however, it is not simply a matter of reaffirming the obvious values of 'cultural heritage' and prescribing the best twenty or forty texts or authors as a way of achieving them, but of more fully understanding the processes involved in 'personal growth'. It is indeed this model as it has become popularly understood from the progressive sixties that has attracted most attention in the representations made to Kingman and Cox about what they should have been setting in place as an alternative. Bullock saw in it the dangers of over-emphasising a child-centred view of education by deliberately exploiting the vagueness of what English is. In this, it is assumed that language learning takes place 'naturally' without intervention by the teacher; the exploration of 'themes' - from filleted extracts of texts - replaces fuller literary study; a too-permissive approach to 'incorrect' English is allowed in the greater interest of developing a confident, personal and individualised way of thinking in non-standard forms; and a 'free' or 'creative' response is encouraged to whatever stimuli can be provided in the classroom. Personal growth is not an entirely subjective process, though, of course, it has to be asserted that the child is at the centre of the educative process. Since learning takes place within a particular culture (regardless of whether or not it is one where social change is an appropriate objective), we have to acknowledge that the individual pupil is not free to grow independently of the society in which he lives. We are what we are because of the experience that we share with others in our present and as a result of what we have inherited from our past. George Steiner understood this well in emphasising the importance of the past in identifying what we are in the present:

Each new historical era mirrors itself in the picture and active mythology of its past or of a past borrowed from other cultures. It tests its sense of identity, of regress or new achievement against the past. The echoes by which a society seeks to determine the reach, the logic and the authority of its own voice, come from the rear. Evidently the mechanisms at work are complex and rooted in diffuse but vital needs of continuity. A society requires antecedents. (Steiner 1975 13).

In such a view, 'cultural heritage' is not an inert body of knowledge which the cultivated few have the obligation to hand on intact to succeeding generations, but is itself actively involved in the formulating processes of defining identity, the value systems and the social objectives of the new. Personal growth, like the growth of society, involves bringing the past into vital relationship with the present, not discarding it. Interestingly, the same point was being made at the Darmouth Conference in the sixties:

Clearly we must recognise the importance of the instinct of origination but an education based on the training of the instinct is not enough. Language conveys to a child an already prepared system of values and ideas that form his culture. Each generation is not a new people; we are what we are because we are able to share a past, in a common heritage, not simply because of our ability to communicate in the present and share the excitement of innovation. (Glyn Lewis 1980).

The real growthof the individual is, as both comments indicate, an adjustment between the private and the public; what sociologists call 'acculturation' is the merging of the individual perception of the 'me' and 'mine' with what is 'ours' and what is shared. In this, the past is as important as the present in the shaping of an independent and personal view of the world.

Since it is, of course, through language that such formulations take place, it is ultimately a pupil's language resources that will determine the quality of the adjustment or growth which takes place. Just as the literature of the past should not be seen as museum pieces to be treasured as relics of a precious inheritance, so, too, language itself must increasingly be understood to be part of that formulating process as the language that we inherit is brought into active interrelationship with the present. T.S. Eliot understood this interrelationship well in expressing his concern about the literacy of contemporary poets in a passage which is interesting here:

What would make me most apprehensive about the future of the language - and that implies the future of sensibility, for what we cease to be able to try to find words for, we cease to be able to feel - would be to observe a decreasing level of literacy among poets. (T. S. Eliot 1939)

As early as 1939, a poet is here suggesting that language is not an inert body of signs and symbols that we impose on to our pre-existing experiences, but is itself an active ingredient in the generating process by which those experiences come into existence. If this is true, then such a comment as this from a poet and not an educationist, is interestingly one of the most powerful arguments against a 'skills' emphasis on teaching that presupposes that syntactical rules, etc can be taught in isolation and then transferred like a matrix on to a body of experience which is nurtured elsewhere in the curriculum. Indeed, it is increased awareness over the years of the close relationship between the acquisition of competence (what Eliot refers to in his proper use of 'literacy') and growth or maturation in the ways in which we build our perceptions of the world, which unites all those concerned with developing pupils' ability in English. It is this understanding that, - wherever teachers have individually placed emphasis in their teaching - language, literature or the cultivation of interests in the wider cultural community outside the school - has characterised good teaching practice over the years and avoided the extremes too glibly aired by those whose disposition is more to label and condemn than properly to investigate what has really been happening in schools. In such practice, no rigid division has ever existed between language and literature in the interrelated nature of teaching which has emphasised the complementarity of the two together, though it has to be acknowledged that it was not until 1985 that this relationship was nationally recognised in the setting up of GCSE English that set out to examine them together in one paper.

If the experience of the literature of the past in the language that contains it plays an important part in contributing to the growth of the individual and the society he inhabits, so, too, does it have a heuristic function. The chapter in the Bullock Report that deals with 'Language and Learning' sums up this process well:

It is a confusion of everyday thought that we tend to regard 'knowledge' as something that exists independently of someone who knows. 'What is known' must be brought to life afresh within every 'knower' by his own efforts. To bring knowledge into being is a formulating process, and language is its ordinary means, whether in speaking or writing, or in the interior monologue of thought. Once it is understood that talking and listening are means of learning those more obvious truths that we learn also from other people by listening and reading fall into a proper perspective. (Bullock 1975, 4.9, 50)

By this process, 'knowledge' is not a commodity to be acquired simply by instruction or being told, or by rote learning. No more is it something which can be 'discovered' - a popular misconception of what is meant by a 'finding out for oneself' or the discovery method of learning. Instead, it is the result of a collaborative process between teacher and taught, a process in which the teacher, from the position of explicit knowledge and understanding of the complexities of the processes involved, actively directs the learning of pupils and leaves nothing to chance.

When the Northern Ireland Report indicates that two of the three principles on which their proposals are based are, first, that English is heuristic, i.e., that it has to do with learning and discovery, and secondly, that it is holistic, - that the four modes of language on which the curriculum is based, reading, writing, speaking and listening are inextricably interwoven, it is building not just on the findings of those reports that immediately preceded it, but on a foundation already firmly laid by Bullock. In the final paragraph of the Chapter 'Language and Learning', Bullock summed up the inferences to be drawn from the important connection he had established between language and learning:

(i)   *all genuine learning involves discovery, and it is as
        ridiculous to suppose that teaching begins and ends
        with 'instruction' as it is to suppose that 'learning by
        discovery' means leaving children to their own devices;*

(ii)   *language has a heuristic function: that is to say a child
        can learn by talking and writing as certainly as he can
        be listening and reading;*

(iii)   *to exploit the process of discovery through all its uses is
        the surest means of enabling a child to master his
        written tongue.*

Indeed it is this latter statement that is repeated practically verbatim in the Northern Ireland Report (Chapter 4:10 , 50). It was, therefore, in the context of how the teacher could best exploit these processes that Bullock demanded greater explicit knowledge of how language function. With regard to his particular remit - the teaching of reading - he writes:

The great majority of teachers are in fact electric in their approach ... The major difference between teachers lies not in their allegiance to a method but in the quality of their relationships with children, their degree of expert knowledge and their sensitivity in matching what they do to each child's current learning needs. (Bullock 1975 Chapter 7:20, 106)

The demand for 'expert knowledge' might seem obvious here, but in any case, it is a vague term that for many might mean no more than the confidence of the teacher in the quality of his own methods. Elsewhere in his Report, however, Bullock made it clear that he had more specific knowledge in mind. For example, in the passage quoted earlier, he described the important place of the development of expressive or personal language for its crucial role in the formulating process by which 'what is known' (knowledge) is brought to life afresh within every knower: it is the means whereby the language in which knowledge is contained is remade within the thinking process of the learner. Talk in the classroom and the teacher's questioning are, therefore, vital to learning: questioning is not simply a means of 'checking' or 'testing' what has been learned, but a means of generating the language by which the learner comes to know it. Commenting on the speed at which questioning often takes place, Bullock wrote:

It is obvious that at this rate of exchange there can be little opportunity for genuine thinking. The teacher's effectiveness will be increased if he has an explicit awareness of the nature and characteristics of the discourse. (Bullock 1975 10:4 p 142)

Equally informed attitudes will enable the teacher to determine when it is appropriate to allow non-standard usage in the classroom - in both speaking and writing - and the purposes for which the discourse in which the pupil is involved will demand that he moves out of his native dialect to communicate more effectively and appropriately in standard English:

During the child's life in the school there should be a gradual and growing extension of his powers of language to met new demands and new situations, and this again takes us firmly to the need for an explicit knowledge by the teacher of how language operates. (Bullock 1975 10:6, 143)

Clearly in the formulating stages of thinking - in the collaborative talk in which pupils engage with other pupils or with the teacher, and in writing some ideas and notes in order to reflect on them and reformulate them - where the emphasis is on the process rather than the product of communication - language closest to the pupils, the language in which he is most comfortable, is the most effective for the task involved. It is at the later stages, that is, where the thinking and reflection have to be further formulated into different kinds of formal discourse structure - for different purposes and audiences - to convey information, knowledge or argument, that the clarity and precision of standard forms assume greater importance and new demands take over. To ensure that pupils can participate fully in all aspects of the language process, they, too, need to have knowledge of the different functions of language and of the various ways in which meaning is communicated.

It was in his emphasis on the need to extend pupils' powers of language to meet these different purposes and functions that Bullock implied that teachers should be able to structure the language activities that they require their pupils to practise. The following passage gives some indication of what that sequence should be:

His development of this ability can be expressed in terms of increasing differentiation. The purposes to which he puts language grow more complex, so that he moves from a narrative level of organising experience to one where he is capable of sustained generalisation. Considered in these terms the handling of language is a complex ability and one that will not be developed simply by working through a series of text-book exercises. (Bullock 1975 1:10, 8)

The question whether stages in language development can be identified and how such a process takes place is a complex issue. Implicit in the new curriculum, which does indeed attempt to define different levels of achievement, is the assumption that some sequence can be planned for, and yet the Northern Ireland Report rightly asserts as the third principle on which its proposals are based that English is recursive:

... that development is often charted not by the acquisition of new skills but by a more sophisticated ability to handle familiar ones. (1989, 1.3, 4)

A great deal of research has been done in the area of how to achieve progress in language development. The work of Inhelder and Piaget, for example, in psychology, as of Vygotsky in his linguistic research, made an important contribution to the thinking of those who, like Bullock and later Kingman, stressed the need for greater awareness by teachers of the important processes involved in language development, stating as they do the important principle on which the new curriculum was ultimately built: namely, that it is not enough that pupils' developing competence in English should be left to chance but that new demands must constantly be made on pupils' language resources if their thinking and learning processes are to grow. There are problems however, in attempting to sequence goals to match the chronological stages of a child's development. On the one hand, to itemise specific tasks in lists can lead to the separation of language skills which are interrelated and recursive. On the other hand, not to attempt it at all can lead to what Geoffrey Summerfield called *'a teaching from hand to mouth, a chronic non-co-ordination of learning and a non-policy of ad-hoc excitements'* (Summerfield (1966). Writing of what he perceives to be the chief fault in the new approaches to English favoured in the sixties, Summerfield referred to the need for a more explicit structuring of language development in his demand for *articulated progression.* Paradoxically in the light of Summerfield's criticism, attempts were being made at the time to provide for greater coherence in English teaching. The Nuffield Foundation Project of 1964 (which became the Schools' Council Programmes in Linguistics and English Teaching) set out to investigate how far new linguistic approaches to language - in this case, in the work of M.A.K. Halliday, Professor of Linguistics at University College, London - could be of help to teachers in planning their curriculum. Most interesting, however, was the work of J.C. Moffett, whose *Teaching the Universe of Discourse* in 1968 must have been one of the earliest attempts to break down the line of progression which Bullock was later to identify as that running from narrative to generalising, from concrete to abstract, or what Bernstein had more generally described as progression from a 'restricted' to an 'elaborated' code. Moffett identifies two 'ladders' of language 'ascent'. The first is the relation of the 'speaker' to his 'audience', the second, the 'speaker's' relationship with his 'subject'. In the first, he places 'reflection' on the first rung: the stage at which the speaker (or writer) is thinking or reflecting to himself. The second is 'conversation', the stage at which he is communicating with a friend or friends in their presence. The third stage is 'correspondence': communication between the speaker and another, known to the speaker but not present; and finally 'publication': where the speaker is communicating with an unknown audience. In the second ladder of ascent, the four stages identified are: recording (what is happening), reporting or narrating (what happened), generalising (what happens) and logical argumentation, theorising or speculating (what could or might happen). The interest in such a model as this is not, of course, in the rigid application of it. Moffett suggests, for example, that progression is linear and that one stage of language use cannot take place until the one before it is mastered, and is quite specific that 'publication' should not be demanded of pupils before the secondary school stage. English is, of course, an cumulative and recursive curriculum, as the Northern Ireland Working Group, like their predecessors, point out. It is, therefore, as absurd to prescribe at what precise stage in the individual's learning one kind of language should be reached as it would be to suggest that any one is abandoned in taking on the next.

What is significant, however, particularly in the light of the Programmes of Study and Attainment targets for the new English curriculum, is the direction that Moffett indicated in his ladders, directions which are helpful, not just in planning a curriculum for the different key stages of pupils' maturation, either in the longer or shorter term, but in determining the sequential direction of any one lesson and in helping to account for the success of any one lesson or series of lessons. If, for example, the teacher has introduced a thematic study of some contemporary or local interest and the pupils are unable to produce genuine responses, relying instead on the ready-made clichés of stereotyped response, is it because they are being asked to engage in generalised accounting without proper preparation? Have they first-hand experience? Would more discussion have helped? Have they been motivated to record and reflect sufficiently on the materials that they have as a result of structured questioning? Without adequate help in the early stages of their response, they have no genuine understanding or knowledge, so that they have no alternative but to report verbatim the 'given': wholesale adoption of the information provided on the chalkboard or copied out from printed resources. The 'formulating process' outlined by Bullock by which what is known is brought to mind afresh within every knower by his own effort through the resources of his own expressive language, has here failed to take place. At this stage, the place of assessment as a proper aid to teaching is important if the teacher is to be able to account for the 'product' of that teaching and identify weaknesses in the collaborative partnerships of the classroom. If, to take another example, problems have arisen in the presentation of the pupil's written response, can the teacher usefully account for these? In the passage quoted below the child, aged 10, has been asked to write the rules for playing football:

My favourite game is football. It is well none all over the world. It is not just a kids Game it is a Gown up Game to there are lots and lots of teams in Britain. There is Liverpool and Exeter City and York City and West Ham United and many more team these team meat up and play against each over it. Ends like 3 V 1 and things like that. This is how you play. You have a field and up each end of the pitch you have a goal. And the field has lines - thing you got to do is score in the goals. I mean you have to tick a ball in the Net and Goal keeper got to you from doing this. You elevan players in each side if you are playing Profesinill. And I'll tell you the Rules. If the ball goes off the pitch it is a throwing. And if you kick some man you have a three kick ... I'll tell you the Brisians and theres a Goalkeeper and these defenders, midfielders, strikers, wings, right Back, half back and there's more too and that how you play football.

The problems with Andrew's writing lie not just in its 'secretarial' skills, though he clearly has difficult with spelling and punctuation.

In tackling these problems, however, the question the teacher must address is whether or not he is being asked to write at a level of exposition for which he has not had adequate preparation. Andrew clearly knows a great deal about football, but is obviously finding it hard to extricate himself from the personal account he is giving. Is he ready to learn how to manipulate the passive voice as a way of avoiding 'Now I'll tell you ...'? Does he know what instructions or rules look like? Has he enough 'models' to learn by? Would a diagram help his explanation? Could he learn about connectives which would enable him to avoid beginning each sentence with 'And', 'And then'? Does he know the 'you' for whom he is writing? He is clearly engaged at the level of 'correspondence, rather than of 'publication'. His spelling suggests that he has derived his knowledge from oral rather than written models. Does he then read enough? These are all important questions and answers can only be found to them if the teacher has enough knowledge about how language must operate in this particular context and about the processes by which Andrew might be brought to manipulate it.

It was not, of course, Bullock's particular brief to provide detailed programmes of study that would illustrate the kind of coherent, structured progression which he had in mind, though as we can see, he pointed valuable signposts for those who succeeded him, in the direction such planning should take. What he did, however, was to caution teachers away from a curriculum made up of short tasks apparently unrelated to what had gone before or what would follow. Equally, he emphasised the importance of providing within the curriculum a broad variety of formats and purposes for language use in which pupils could actively collaborate with one another and with the teacher in a community of language users that would ensure development or competence in the four modes: reading, writing, speaking and listening. These should be taught in an interrelated way and developed from the contexts in which pupils experienced language: first, in the context of English as a discrete subject within the curriculum with a specific emphasis on literature; secondly, in the heuristic and cross-curricular aspects of English as a means of acquiring knowledge and skill in other subjects; thirdly, in all the contexts in which language skill is necessary to develop social competence; and last, in all the contexts in which pupils encounter language in their cultural environment, in newspapers, brochures and in the media in general. Formal 'correctness' should be taught, but only when it arises out of the contexts of learning in which pupils are involved and in the process of formulating appropriate responses to them.

In support of his demand for greater knowledge on the part of the teacher, Bullock also made specific recommendations that a special language course should form part of the English teacher's education course and that, in turn, the expertise of the English teacher should be acknowledged and exploited in the school context, in the appointment of a language co-ordinator whose role would be to devise a language policy for the school in collaboration with colleagues and to advise and guide, not just on the cross-curricular aspects of the subject, but on attitudes to matters like 'correctness'. These recommendations - together with many others contained in *A Language for Life* - were not implemented on any large scale, partly, one suspects, because the benign voice of the author allowed too many teachers within his audience to respond only to those parts of the report that endorsed their own practices and partly because Bullock did not offer the government of the day - in whose hands and purse a full implementation lay - the solutions they wanted to hear. Interestingly, however, in Northern Ireland, the response to the report was otherwise. A genuine attempt was made to formulate a rationale for language learning in the *Language and Literacy Guideline for Primary Schools*, set up by the Northern Ireland Council for Educational Development in 1985. In addition, many primary schools went on to appoint a Language Co-ordinator (though it has to be acknowledged not all are English specialists).

It was not, however, until the DES produced their pamphlet, *English from 5 to 16*, in the HMI *Curriculum Matters* Series in 1984, that an attempt was made to produce a document which set out a sequenced programme indicating the language skills which pupils should be able to achieve at specific stages from 5 to 16 within the English curriculum. The twenty-two page document was too short to contain the detailed rationale that was necessary to explain the articulated progression which underlay the specific demands made at the three key stages they identified - at age 7, 11, 16. Few, however, could have disagreed with the general statement made in the introduction, outlining three aims for the interacting modes of speaking, reading and writing, which closely echoed Bullock. It was the addition of a fourth aim, which applied over all the modes of language, which caused the trouble already referred to in the introduction to this essay:

This is to teach pupils about language, so that they achieve a working knowledge of its structure and of the variety of ways in which meaning is made, so that they have a vocabulary for discussing it, so that they can use it with greater awareness, and because it is interesting. (Chapter 1:6, 3)

For many, who had perhaps not read Bullock carefully, this 'new' demand seemed to contradict *A Language for Life* in pointing to return to a 'grammar grind' model of English and a denial of the more 'creative' approaches to the subject developed from the sixties. For others, it was demanding a knowledge that they did not themselves possess, and it was to redeem this latter concern that Kingman was invited to make his proposals. The importance of *English 5 to 16* in formulating the new curriculum for English, should not be underestimated, however.

The Kingman Report, narrower as it was in its remit, is a much fuller and more explicit statement of what teachers need to know about language than Bullock had provided. Like Bullock, however, Kingman's Report emphasises the need for an incremental growth of language provided for in situations of increasingly complex demand, through which pupils would be enabled

... to perceive patterns in their experience, to give an account (if only to themselves) of the world as they perceive it and to recognise other, perhaps conflicting accounts. Increasing control of otherwise undifferentiated experience is thereby achieved, so leading children towards the linguistic capacities of adulthood ... (Kingman 1988, 2:13, 9)

The Kingman Report recognises and acknowledges the important contribution Bullock made in emphasising the vital connection to be made between language and thinking in the intellectual and cognitive development of pupils, enabling them through the formulating processes in which they experience language to encounter the thoughts, hypotheses, explanations and analyses of the greatest human minds. Kingman would include the greatest works of literature in such a developmental process, the language of literature enabling pupils both to order their own experience and to discover new feelings and experiences through the best that is contained in their cultural heritage.

An important addition made by Kingman refocused the efforts of those teachers of the sixties and seventies to bring issues of social concern into the curriculum in the form of 'thematic' study. Apart from the obvious danger of reducing English teaching to a form of political dogmatising, Kingman rightly points out (as Bullock had done) the limitation of turning the English classroom into a forum for the rehearsal of half-formed or partially-understood moral or social issues, however important the generation of expressive language or formal argument (the stated aims of many who practised such methods) in the development of linguistic competence.

Nevertheless, modern critical theory was showing that the English classroom could not be seen entirely as a value-free workshop where reading and response to literature and the exercise of the many linguistic skills that made up the curriculum could be practised independently of the cultural environment which surrounded it. Kingman pointed to the revolution brought about by the new 'science' of literary theory - undertaken by the Swiss structuralist de Saussure in the 1920's and culminating in the work of post-structuralists like Barthes, Derrida and Lacan, who demonstrated that no language act nor our responses to it - whether it is a poem or menu, a primitive myth or a modern advertisement, exists independently of cultural or ideological assumption. The implication for teachers, is that they have to think critically about their own ideological assumptions in directing the language activities of English, using language itself as an important resource in the study of the environment we live in and the culture we inhabit. It is in widening the definition of language study in the classroom that Kingman (as Bullock had in his earlier context) makes a rigid distinction between what he means by 'knowledge about language' and the narrow interpretation made by those who suppose that it is acquired by a straightforward learning of grammatical rules. Language is not an inert body of knowledge nor a kit that can be manipulated neutrally for the conveying of information. It can trigger emotional responses that may spring from prejudice, stereotyping or misunderstanding, which newspapers, advertisements, the language of the media in general and the rhetoric of politics, seek to exploit. Such responses occur in attitudes to spoken language, in our reactions to accent, dialect, gender and race. It is the implications of such considerations which teachers of English need to take account of in their teaching. By gaining greater knowledge of language themselves - its history and its historical and regional variations, - Kingman rightly emphasises that pupils can become more actively involved in studying it themselves, gain greater insight into its workings, use it with greater awareness, and respond to it with increased sensitivity and understanding. The Inspectorate 5-16 booklet claimed that such study was interesting itself. That view was thoroughly supported by Kingman, and the new curricula for England, Wales and Northern Ireland endorse it in their programmes of study.

It follows, then, that if, besides an understanding of the importance of language as the medium through which learning takes place, language is also a subject of study in its own right, teachers and pupils require a language in which to discuss its usage. It is in both contexts that Kingman in his report included knowledge of forms of language as an important part of his 'model', demonstrating in the examples he gives how knowledge of the sounds and letters of words and of phrase and sentence structures might promote greater understanding of the grammar of meaning in the various discourse structures in which they are to be used in the classroom. For example, a knowledge of terms is needed to help teachers differentiate between varieties of language, in particular, of course, between spoken and written forms in the range of tasks that pupils are required to perform in language: engaging in small group collaborative discussion in the learning process, the presentation of formal reports, explaining and persuading, giving instructions, writing narrative, description or argument. Terms are required for these different speech acts (to argue a case is not the same as to engage in conversational argument), for the requirements of different audiences in the circumstances and occasions in which they occur, and for the different kinds of direct and indirect meanings that are communicated through inference, presupposition, connotative and emotive language, irony and innuendo. Far from such knowledge imposing a content-based straightjacket on to the English curriculum, learning about the different forms by which meaning is carried enables pupils to appreciate that, as learners, they are not simply gaining access to one language but to many, in all the activities of the English curriculum. Above all, they are gaining a wide repertoire of 'voices' from which they themselves may make deliberate choices in a widening community of language users, by determining the form and style appropriate to purpose and audience in their spoken and written communications.

It is against this background that one of the most controversial demands of the new curriculum needs to be understood: that is, by the end of the key stage 4 pupils should be able to use standard English, as the Northern Ireland Report puts it, 'when the context requires' In order to implement this demand, it is necessary that teachers and pupils know what is meant by 'standard' English recognise the difference between 'accent', which refers specifically to pronunciation, and 'dialect' - a version of English with a vocabulary and grammar specific to the region in which it is spoken and perhaps also written. Standard English is indeed itself a dialect, developed from one of the Middle English dialects of the East Midlands and one that assumed importance because it was the one adopted by Caxton in printing and thus became the first written form of English and subsequently, therefore, the one most readily available to all users of the language whatever region they came from and whatever dialect they spoke. It is the fact of its being the first published form that established it as 'standard', not in the sense of being superior (the main cause of the controversy surrounding it), but because it was the one dialect which language users could share, hence the one in which knowledge came to be transacted, and consequently the language of the education system, the language of published writing and therefore the international language in which business, law, financial and political negotiation takes place. Regional dialects are, by virtue of the fact that they are the shared language of particular geographical regions, of immense value in communicating within the community of users but restricted nevertheless by their vocabulary and the range of their linguistic utterance outside it, just as standard English was in its original dialect form. Because the purposes to which standard English has been put have extended its vocabulary and usage into a wide range of communicated forms, it has become a more elaborated language and it is for this reason that denial of access to it may also inhibit and restrict the users of a local or regional dialect that pupils must be taught to use it. Dialects, of course, enrich the language and understanding of their variety - comparing, for example, the vocabulary and idiom of different parts of the country - can enhance our understanding of the environment in which we live just as much as knowing about its geography or history. Standard English is a vital amenity, however, not because it is superior to the local dialect, but because it enables movement from one region to another and is important to pupils in the processes of learning how to negotiate their own affairs in the wider world of knowledge, commerce or industry to which they seek ultimate access. It should not be assumed, however, that standard English is a fixed form of language answerable to a single set of grammatical 'rules', or that it can be manipulated 'best' or most 'correctly' in the spoken form in only one accent - Received Pronunciation, the accent of Oxford English, or the accent once favoured almost exclusively by the BBC. Since its desired use is to enable wider and clearer communication with audiences who do not share the vocabulary and grammatical structure of the regional dialect, it follows that standard English can be spoken in a variety of accents. Equally, its grammar is not a fixed matrix that, applied to any written or spoken utterance, will render its meaning clear and universally understood. Standard English has many forms which depend on the culture from which they spring. American standard English is one such form. When the President of the United states says in a television interview or speech, 'Next week, I'm in Moscow, then in London', he is not disobeying the 'rule' for the formation of the future tense, but using an American standard form. Indeed, suggestions are bring made in some quarters that the American standard form may well replace the Received Pronunciation of spoken standard English as the preferred language in which to 'get on', a result not just of the super-power image of the United States but also from the fact that so much of the knowledge of technological, medical and other research has expanded American English in the way in which standard English once expanded the dialect of the native language from which it sprang. Since so much of that knowledge is now shared through oral transactions - by TV, video and by a mobile workforce of conference-goers - it is not surprising that its effect is felt not just in England but in Europe as well. Despite the efforts of a French Academy to preserve the vigour of a standardised French, the import of American English has modified spoken and written French in ways which French purists find alarming. What has to be emphasised here is that pupils need to be made aware of language variety of this sort and of the ways in which language changes over time. They need to understand that when the American President speaks in a non-standard English, but in American standard, he is deliberately choosing a language that, in his judgement, may help in establishing friendly relationships with his audience. When he writes a report of the trip to Moscow, however, he will choose another, just as when the results are finally enshrined in the formal language of a legal document, it will subscribe to the conventions and structures of a form which are standard for that kind of communication. Pupils need to learn about these different conventions and that purpose and audience must determine the choices they make.

In making such teaching explicit within the English curriculum, Kingman, Cox and the Northern Ireland Committee stress that knowledge about language should not be 'bolted on' to the curriculum but should be integrated into the three profile components of speaking and listening, reading and writing and this is how it appears in the programmes of Study for Northern Ireland. Professor Cox justified teaching pupils about language not just because it had positive effects on their own language usage but because of the general value of such knowledge as part of their social and cultural environment. The new cultural awareness he was advocating had to take account of an increasingly multi-racial society where greater understanding, not just of the indigenous dialects, but also of different creoles of English and the history and development of these languages, can create respect for other cultures and a greater appreciation of their cultural interaction within society. The presence of bilingual children in English should be seen as an additional resource rather than a restriction to the linguistic development of native speakers, particularly in the light of increased labour mobility and greater cultural contact within the European Community after 1992. In Northern Ireland, where the resources available to a multi racial-society do not exist, understanding our language and the particular dialects which make it up is justified from a slightly different concept of mutual understanding but one of no less importance. In Northern Ireland, language is both a tool and a weapon, where dialectal difference can be seen as a mark of cultural and religious division that has its roots in a violent past and, sadly, an equally violent present. Here, understanding of English, its local dialects and the history from which they spring, is offered as a way of exploring our cultural heritage, which might provide a valuable means of bridging differences through the common cultural past which we share. In such work, pupils' own knowledge and experience may well be the source of 'expertise' within the classroom, where collecting and classifying of vocabulary and dialectal difference, learning the methodology of observation, description, explanation and hypothesis-making, can lead to a comparative study that is far removed from the learning of an inert 'body of knowledge' and which can establish a sense of sameness within a divided community as much as difference. Interestingly, appeal to the cultural heritage of the nation as a way of achieving mutual understanding, is now new nor exclusive to those who devised these cross-curricular themes. W.B. Yeats, at the beginning of the century, aimed to unite division within the island by initiating a Literary Movement and poetic theatre that drew on the myth and legend of the common 'memory of the race' for its metaphor and image. The fact that Yeats' aim foundered did not detract from the value of the effort and the point is made here, not to draw attention to the possibility of failure in the Northern Ireland aim, but simply to show that educationists and poets are often closer in their thinking about the value of their subject than many suppose.

Little specific reference has been made in this chapter to the particular problems raised by the vexed question of assessment and testing in English, partly because there are issues that have yet to be resolved and because, in any case, it is too large an area to be addressed here. National testing aat 8, 11, 14 and 16 years is, however, generally thought to have been a new idea conceivable only by a Conservative government whose obsession is with market forces, competitiveness and accountability within the profession and that little can be achieved by public monitoring of what goes on in schools. Clearly confusion exists between the declared intention of providing proper diagnostic assessment of the progress of individual children, measured against professionally-determined norms and inter-school 'ratings', and it remains to be seen whether the two can be successfully reconciled within a single system. As far as English is concerned, it should be remembered however, that Bullock, in 1975 and Kingman, in 1985, both advocated formal assessment, the only difference being that, where Bullock suggested age eleven as the earliest stage where it should occur, Kingman recommended age seven as the first stage at which teachers should be able to identify those areas of language acquisition where pupils might need help. Indeed, Kingman went so far as to suggest that to defer such diagnosis until a later stage might be to leave it too late. Both Bullock and Kingman saw assessment as a proper aid to teaching and the Task Groups on assessment and testing concur with them in insisting that it should not determine what is taught and learned, nor be bolted on as an additional curriculum demand, but should be integral to the learning process, continually providing the feed-back and feed-forward that teachers need if they are to provide effective learning experience based on the successes and failures of the procedures of the past. (Yeats 1967 p113)

The particular problems raised by national monitoring through standardised tests of whatever kind focuses attention once more on the foundation on which a national curriculum in English is built and poses the ultimate question of whether a linear sequence of language development can be articulated in such a way that we can accurately determine the stages by which pupils should be able to perform specific tasks in speaking, reading and writing. The Northern Ireland committee, in common with their counterparts in England, rightly emphasise repeatedly in their rationale, the recursive nature of the subject, and demonstrate this in the broad terms in which the Programmes of Study are described, programmes that properly take account of variations between individual pupils in the sequences on which the three profile components are followed. The danger of destroying the holistic nature of the subject emphasised by Bullock in the integrated and interrelated ways in which the different language moves should be practised if a continuous and effective way of learning is to take place, should not detract, however, from the need to make this process more explicit. The value of such explicitness for parents, for teachers in other schools and for individual teachers themselves, should not be underestimated.

The rationale that underlies the new curriculum for English is not a manifesto for a revolutionary new model for English, which is why the responses to it from so many teachers both here and in England have been so positive, many finding in it the support for the good practice in teaching and assessment that fortunately now, as in the past, has managed to resist and transcend all the pressures from those on the right and left of the political spectrum to shape it to their own purpose. The new curriculum answers the demands of those who continue to favour a 'personal growth' view of English, by continuing to insist on the centrality of the child in the learning process whose end is a personally-informed, independent view of the world, while simultaneously emphasising the responsibility of English teachers to prepare their pupils for the language demands of adult life. It acknowledges, too, the centrality of the subject in a cross-curricular perspective, demonstrating the close relationship that exists between language and learning in all subjects. It includes the 'cultural heritage' view of the subject, by stressing the responsibility of schools to lead pupils to an appreciation of those works of literature that have been widely regarded as among the finest in the language, but extends this view by including, within that heritage, texts in English written from the perspective of other cultures. It adds a further perspective to the 'cultural heritage' and 'skills' approach to English by including language itself as an important subject for study both in a historical perspective and present-day usage, knowledge and understanding of which will promote greater tolerance of and sensitivity to those whose language and experience are different from ours. It argues convincingly that the whole of the English curriculum in the skills and values that it promotes is a potent force in developing mutual understanding, not only in multi-cultural and multi-racial societies, but more urgently in the divided community of Northern Ireland that our children have inherited.

It is often supposed that English teachers are by nature resistant to change. Where scientists work in groups, talking collaboratively on a research project whose relevance is to a future world, literary scholarship is a more private endeavour, an engagement between a solitary reader and the interior world of a book, the ultimate value of which is, as Yeats ironically described it, *wasteful virtues* (Yeats 1967). Many have resented attempts to bring these private and secret activities of English into the arena of public debate and scrutiny. But it was one of the beneficial effects of GCSE, for example, that English teachers were drawn into working more closely with one another, engaging in lively debate about the criteria by which competence in the subject could be defined and measured. The publication of a national curriculum for the subject, emphasising a continuous progression in pupils' language development from primary to secondary levels of schooling, now draw primary teachers into the discussion that is already taking place at the higher level. For the first time, the question 'What is English?' which in the past decade has been debated mainly in the more rarified forum of the universities and worked out in the advancement of more and more branches of literary theory, has become the concern of all those engaged in the teaching of the subject. It can only be hoped, therefore, that the next change in curriculum matters relating to English will be generated from within the profession and not imposed on it from without.

POSTSCRIPT

Leslie Caul

During the course of the preparation of this book two major themes emerged. First, the change from a partnership model of curriculum development based on open discussion to a new model where the content of the curriculum was defined by central government and made operational in schools. This model includes a complex mode of accountability that has already been breached by Secretaries of State who have chosen to change the curriculum by arbitrary decision. Second, the degree of secrecy involved and the growing control of decision making through manipulation rather than open discussion and public debate. This book however sets out the educational basis of the curriculum from a theoretical and from a practical perspective. It puts the debates about the Common Curriculum into the educational and therefore public domain where it can be further analysed for future discussion about education in the province.

The 'secret garden' of curriculum, nevertheless, has been well and truly 'smashed' by demands for centralised control by government and the need it identified for improved academic outcomes in schools. In this context can the legitimate desires of teachers for professional autonomy be reconciled with the wider demands for public accountability? The evidence regarding educational outcomes in Northern Ireland display a need for improvement in the secondary education sector. There has been a long unmet political need for some kind of centralised system of curriculum planning to improve standards that will not amount to central control. This has clearly not been achieved except for the power available to the various examination boards who exercise considerable authority at key stage 4. If the state compels children to attend school for 10-11 years it has a duty to ensure that the time spent at school is worthwhile. Contemporary curriculum in Northern Ireland demands that standards are adhered to with the introduction of regular assessment and explicit control of the content of the knowledge to be transmitted in schools.

The present model for national curriculum is based on the ideas that the centre can set out the broad outline for schooling but that this framework should be delivered in ways accepted by a broad consensus among teachers. The teachers' case is that they as a professional group should be at the centre of decision making about the curriculum. These two positions, centralised control and the professional autonomy of teachers are at the centre of a set of tensions about the common curriculum.

The Northern Ireland curriculum can be seen to reflect the nature and content of its cross curricular themes. In these themes the curriculum develops a mirror image of the divided nature of the province through its use of EMU and Cultural Heritage. The themes may be seen to be in opposition as they seek to unify and yet identify the divisions in Northern Ireland. Discussion of their utility throws into sharp relief the possibilities for education as a powerful force for reconciliation while simultaneously identifying potential difficulties. In Northern Ireland the last thing children need is a reminder of their cultural heritage and their ethnic identity. If education is to alleviate problems of identity considerable attention must be given to methodology in schools. Just how can a system of education contribute to the lessening of community tensions is an important educational question. However in this age of an emerging Europe schools in Northern Ireland have pioneered much work of this type.

Core issues in the Common Curriculum have their roots in debates about numeracy and literacy. Both in mathematics and English vigorous debates have searched for a 'holy grail', a fundamental approach to the teaching of these subjects. As argued in this book the mathematics and the English curriculum in Northern Ireland reflect these debates. IT, Economic Awareness and in science on the other hand reflect core debates that are less theoretical and related to the practical concerns of the classroom teacher. Even here the curriculum in Northern Ireland has pioneered good work in new initiatives in the school.

The introduction of the Common Curriculum has made teachers' tasks more difficult and complex. In this new age of reform and internal market forces within education the successful delivery of the common curriculum may be the price of professionalism. Teaching in this age involves the delivery of a centrally defined body of knowledge and skills. Local and professional autonomy is a thing of the past. It is up to all the teaching profession to make the Common Curriculum a worthwhile enterprise. Now that it is at last in place the system must begin to set up machinery for curriculum development if the early gains of the innovation are not to be lost. It is now time for the development of a shared control of curriculum between schools and the government, a control that reflects in the legitimate interests of those who will deliver the goals of the province's education service. Within this context this book attempts to clarify the philosophy behind the Common Curriculum in order to make public the basis of a Northern Ireland curriculum and to begin a debate about the values inherent in education in the province.

BIBLIOGRAPHY

Assessment of Performance Unit (1981) *Personal Social Development*, DES: London.

Baldwin, J. and Wells, H. (1979) *Active Tutorial Work: years 1-5*, Blackwell: Oxford.

Becket J.C. (1966) *The Making Of Modern Ireland*, Faber, London.

Bourdieu P & Passeron J.C. (1977) *Reproduction in Education, Society and Culture*, Sage, London.

Broadfoot, P et al (1989) Records of achievement: Report of the National Evaluation of Pilot Schemes in Murphy, P. and Moon, B. *Developments in Learning and Assessment*, Hodden and Stoughton, London.

Bullick, E.H.A. (1990) Education Beyond Enmity, unpublished M.A. Dissertation, University of Ulster at Magee.

Bullock, A . (1975) *A Language for Life:* Report of the Committee of Inquiry appointed by the Secretary of State for Education and Science under the Chairmanship of Sir Alan Bullock, (HMSO).

Burrage, H. (1987) Sociology and Health Education in *The Curriculum, Social Science Teacher* 17,1, pp19-20.

Cameron Report (1969) "Disturbances in Northern Ireland"*Cmd.* 532 HMSO Belfast.

Cathcart, R. (1984) *The Most Troublesome Region*, Blackstaff, Belfast.

Caul, L. (1990) *Schools Under Scrutiny: The case of Northern Ireland.* MacMillan Educational, London.

Cockcroft, W.H. (1982) Mathematics Counts (Report of the Committee of Inquiry into the Teaching of Mathematics in Schools) HMSO London.

Corrnelius, M. (1985) From Jeffery Syllabus to Cockcroft Report (part 2) *Mathematics in School*, November, 1985, pp28-30.

Cowan, A.M. (1990) Injustice, Antagonism and the Deformation of Conversation, background paper for Lifespring Health and Healing Summer Programme, Belfast.

Cox, J. (1991) *Cox on Cox: an English Curriculum for the 1990s*, Hodder and Stoughton, London,

Cranny, P. (1990) Three Small Schools Together: Towards Education for Mutual Understanding, unpublished report ED 510, Faculty of Education, UUC.

Crone, R. and Malone, J. (1979) *Continuities in Education: the Northern Ireland Schools Curriculum Project*, NFER. Slough.

Crone, R. and Malone, J. (1983) *The Human Curriculum*, Farset Co-operative Press, Belfast.

Cutbert, E. (1990) *EMU in the Primary Curriculum: an Evaluation*, University of Ulster at Coleraine.

Cullen, B. and McGuffin, S.J. (1989) The Effectiveness of the Northern Ireland teaching package on AIDS Awareness, First European Conference on Effectiveness of Health Education, Rotterdam.

Department of Education , Northern Ireland (1981) *Primary Education* (Report of an Inspectorate Survey in Northern Ireland) DENI, Bangor.

Department of Education, Northern Ireland (1982) The Improvement of Community Relations: the Contribution of Schools. *Circular 1982/21* DENI, Bangor.

Department of Education, Northern Ireland (1987)
Cross-community Contact Scheme, *Circular 1987/47* DENI,
Bangor.

Department of Education, Northern Ireland (1988)
Cross-community Contact Scheme - Education for Mutual
Understanding, *Circular 1988/2* DENI, Bangor.

Department of Education, Northern Ireland (1988) *Education in
Northern Ireland - proposals for reform*, DENI, Bangor.

Department of Education, Northern Ireland (1989a.)
Cross-community Contact Scheme, *Circular 1989.*

Department of Education, Northern Ireland (1989b.) *Education
for Mutual Understanding:* A Cross-Curricular Theme, *Report of the
Working Group on Education for Mutual Understanding*,
Rathgael House, Bangor.

Department of Education, Northern Ireland (1989) Health
Education A cross curricular theme, *Consultation Paper*, DEN,
Bangor.

Department of Education, Northern Ireland (1989) Information
Technology; A cross curricular theme, *Consultation Paper*, DENI,
Bangor.

Department of Education, Northern Ireland (1990) *Aspects of
provision in Education in Northern Ireland 1987-1989: a report by the
Inspectorate*, DENI: Bangor.

**Department of Education and Science and the Welsh Office
(1985)** *GCSE: The National Criteria (Mathematics)* HMSO, London.

Department of Education and Science (1977) *Health Education
in Schools*, HMSO, London.

Dixon, J. (1967) *Growth through English*, NATE, Huddersfield.

Dixon, J. (1975) *Growth through English: Set in the Perspective of the Seventies*, Oxford Studies in Education, 3rd edition, Open University Press.

Eastern Health and Social Services Board/NICED (1988) *AIDS Education for Schools*, EHSSB/NICED: Belfast, York.

Eliot, T.S. (1939) 'That Poetry is made with Words', *New English Weekly*, XV No. 2, 27 April, 1939.

English from 5 to 16, Curriculum Matters I, (1984.) An HMI Series, HMSO, London

Evans, E.E. (1970) *The Personality of Ulster*, Transactions of the Institute of Geographers.

Fiske R. (1985) *In Time of War* Paladin, London.

Foster R. (1989) *Modern Ireland 1600-1972*, London: Penguin.

Freudenberg, N. (1981) Health Education for Social Change: a strategy for public health in the US. *International Journal of Health Education* 24 (3) pp 1-8.

Greer, J. and McElhinney, E.P. (1984) The Project on Religion in Ireland: an Experiment in Reconstruction, *Lumen Vitae*, 39 3.

Health Education Council (1984) *My Body*, Heinemann London.

Health Education Council (1986) *Natural Nashers*, Drake Cardiff.

Health Education Council (undated) *Schools Health Education Project 5-13: a training manual*, HEC London.

Houlton, P., Murphy, M.J., Majuire, J., and Boyd, S. (1976) Reports on Schools Council Projects: Health Education 5-13. *Northern Ireland Schools Curriculum Committee: News Bulletin* 20, pp3-7.

Irvine, R. (1988) Health related fitness in the secondary school: Physical Education Programmes, NICED *Core* pp 6-7.

Kingman, J. (1988) Report of the Committee of Inquiry into the Teaching of English Language, HMSO, London.

Lecky, E. (1989) Preparing for Education for MutualUnderstanding in School, unpublished report ED 510, Faculty of Education, University of Ulster at Coleraine.

Lewis, G. (1969) 'The Teaching of English', p.2. (Working Party IV) Dartmouth Seminar Papers, NCTE, 1969, quoted in David Allen, English Teaching since 1965: *How Much Growth?*, Heinemann, London.

Lyons, F.S.L. (1971) *Ireland Since The Famine*, Fontana London.

Magee, J. (1970) The Teaching of Irish History in Irish Schools *The Northern Teacher*, Winter.

McEwen, A. et al (1985) Subject Choices at A Level in Northern Ireland *European Journal of Science Education*, 8,1 39-49.

McGuffin, S. (1983) Health Knowledge and Behaviour of Young People, *Monograph No.5*, HEC: London.

McGuffin, S. (1976) Health Education in Northern Ireland- a survey of current practice in post primary schools, *Journal, Institute of Health Education*, 14, 1, pp 20-26.

McIntosh, A. (1977) When Will They Ever Learn? *Forum*, vol 19 No. 3.

McKeown, T. and Lowe, C.R. (1974) *An Introduction to Social Medicine*, Blackwell Oxford.

Moffett, J.C. (1968) *Teaching the Universe of Discourse*, Houghton Mifflin Co., Boston, J.C.

National Curriculum Council (1988) *Consultation Report: Science,* NICC York

Northern Ireland Certificate of Secondary Education (1981) *Rules and Schemes of Examination 1983,* NISEC, Belfast.

Northern Ireland Certificate of Secondary Education (1982) *Rules and Schemes of Examination 1984,* NISEC, Belfast.

Northern Ireland Council for Educational Development (1983) *Health Education Guidelines for Primary Schools,* NICED, Belfast.

Northern Ireland Council for Educational Development (1983) *Health Education within the Curriculum 5-19,* NICED, Belfast.

Northern Ireland Council for Educational Development (1984) *Mathematics Guidelines for Primary Schools,* Stranmillis College, Belfast.

Northern Ireland Council for Educational Development (1988) *Education for Mutual Understanding: a Guide,* NICED, Bangor.

Northern Ireland Curriculum Council (1989) *Cross-Curricular Themes,* NICC, Stranmillis College, Belfast.

Northern Ireland Curriculum Council (1990) *Mathematics Guidance Material,* Stranmillis College, Belfast.

Northern Ireland Curriculum Council (1990) *Science Guidance Material,* Stranmillis College, Belfast.

Northern Ireland Schools Examination Council (1986) *General Certificate of Secondary Education Examination 1988: Mathematics,* Belfast.

O'Donnell, E.E. (1977) *Northern Irish Stereotypes,* Institute of Public Services, Dublin.

Pring, R. (1984) *Personal and Social Education in the Curriculum,* Hodder and Stoughton London.

Rice, B. (1981) *Informal Methods in Health and Social Education* TACADE: Manchester.

Robinson, A. (1983) The Schools Cultural Studies Project: a Contribution to Peace in Northern Ireland, *Director's Report,* New University of Ulster, Coleraine.

Secondary Science Curriculum Review (1987) *Better Science: Health and Social Education (curriculum guide 9),* Hieinemann, London.

Schools Council (1976) *Health Education in Secondary Schools* (Working Paper 57) Evans/Methuen, London.

Schools Council (1979) *Home and Family 8-13: Planning for home and family,* Forbes: London.

Schools Council 'Health Education 5-13 Project' (1977) *All about me: Teachers Guide Early Years of Schooling (5-8),* Nelson, Walton on Thames.

Schools Council/Health Education Council (1980) *Health Education 13-18 Developing Health Education: A Co-ordinators Guide,* Forbes, London.

Scottish Health Education Group (1986) The Health Promoting School: Report of Symposium, Pebbles.

Smith, A. and Dunn, S. (1990) Expending Inter-School Links, Centre for the Study of Conflict, University of Ulster, Coleraine.

Steiner, G. (1975) *In Bluebeard's Castle,* Faber, London.

Summerfield, G. (1966) 'Great Expectations', *New Education,* 2m, 3, March.

Tones, K. (1987) Health Promotion, Affective Education and the Personal Social Development of Young People in David, K. and

Tones, K., Tilford, S. and Robinson, Y.K. (1990) *Health Education effectiveness and efficiency*, Chapman and Hall London.

Vygotsky, L.S (1962) *Thought and Language*, Massachusetts Institute of Technology Press, Cambridge, Mass.

Williams, T. (1987) Health Education in Secondary Schools In David, K. and Williams,T. (ed) *Health Education in Schools*, Harper and Row: London.

Williams,T. and Williams, N. (1981) *Personal and Social Development in the Curriculum*, SCHEP Southampton.

Wilson, D. and Dunn, S. (1989) *Integrated Schools: Information for parents*, Centre for the Study of Conflict, University of Ulster at Coleraine.

World Health Organisation (1984) *Health Promotion: a discussion of the concept and principles*, WHO, Copenhagen.

World Health Organisation (1987) *Health Promotion: concept and principles in action: a policy framework*, WHO, Copenhagen.

Young, I, (1990) Personal Communication *: Draft Paper*, Scottish Health Education Group.